Technology, Culture and Communication

D0024185

The media have a huge impact on how we view society and the world, and new technologies continue to transform the way in which we work and learn. It is therefore essential that young people can engage critically in their consumption of media and the Internet and are able to make informed decisions about the technologies they use.

This book explores the broad contexts and ideas that technology facilitates in our culture and considers what this means for teachers in practice. It aims to help you develop your understanding about, and pedagogy with, technology and includes:

- the implications of new media and technology on twenty-first-century education;
- guidance on choosing and using digital technologies and how these affect the educational opportunities for young people;
- a consideration of students' critical and creative thinking with digital media and their confidence and autonomy in digital consumption and production;
- references to recent research to support practice;
- links to resources and organisations who can offer support.

Technology has a crucial role to play in processes of teaching and learning. This book is essential reading for trainee and practising teachers who wish to use a range of technological tools to form a dynamic and creative learning environment.

Jonathan Savage is Reader in Education and Enterprise Fellow at the Institute of Education, Manchester Metropolitan University. He is also a Visiting Research Fellow at the Royal Northern College of Music. He teaches on various PGCE courses and doctoral studies programmes and is an active researcher in a wide range of areas relating to education and ICT.

Clive McGoun is Senior Lecturer in Communication at Manchester Metropolitan University. His wide-ranging teaching and research interests include digital media communications and the culture and political economy of Web 2.0.

Teaching contemporary themes in secondary education series

The secondary National Curriculum encourages teachers to develop more creative and flexible teaching around interrelated themes, which will help young people to make sense of some of the key ideas and challenges in today's world.

This series explores the key themes of global learning and sustainable development, creativity and critical thinking, technology and the media, identity and cultural diversity, and enterprise.

Each theme represents a key topic considered to be of particular relevance to young people growing up in the twenty-first century. These themes are not intended to be curriculum subjects, but rather over-arching themes that bring a greater sense of relevance and interconnectedness to the way in which young people learn.

These books aim to explore such themes in some depth, investigating how they link to different areas of the curriculum (including different education agendas) while giving an overview of policy changes and implications for practice. They provide ideas on how to incorporate these themes through a whole-school approach, using practical case studies of a range of activities and approaches, with detailed information on how this was organised and implemented and the outcomes and learning achieved.

About the editors

Helen Gadsby is the course leader for the PGCE secondary geography course at Liverpool Hope University. She also teaches on the BAQTS and PGCE primary courses. She has 16 years' teaching experience in secondary schools, where she held positions of Head of Geography and Head of Year. Helen's research interests include education for sustainable development and global learning. She has presented workshops and papers around these topics at a number of national and international conferences.

Andrea Bullivant works for Liverpool World Centre, an organisation that works with schools, communities and organisations to raise awareness about issues of global interdependence and global justice. As part of this role she has worked closely with the Education Faculty at Liverpool Hope University to embed global learning within LHU's teacher training and education courses. More recently this work has involved developing CPD training for teachers on global learning themes and supporting the work of LHU's Centre for International and Development Education (CfIDE).

Technology, Culture and Communication

Jonathan Savage and Clive McGoun

LONDON AND NEW YORK

First published 2012
by Routledge
2 Park Square, Milton Park, Abingdon, Oxon OX14 4RN

Simultaneously published in the USA and Canada
by Routledge
711 Third Avenue, New York, NY 10017

Routledge is an imprint of the Taylor & Francis Group, an informa business

© 2012 Jonathan Savage and Clive McGoun

British Library Cataloguing in Publication Data
A catalogue record for this book is available from the British Library

Library of Congress Cataloging in Publication Data
McGoun, Clive.
Teaching contemporary themes in secondary education : technology, culture and communication / Clive McGoun and Jonathan Savage.
     p. cm.
     1. Educational technology. 2. Media literacy--Study and teaching. I. Savage, Jonathan. II. Title.
     LB1028.3.M393 2011   371.33--dc23
     2011043696

ISBN: 978–0–415–62030–7 (hbk)
ISBN: 978–0–415–62031–4 (pbk)
ISBN: 978–0–203–12144–3 (ebk)

Typeset in Bembo and Helvetica Neue
by Bookcraft Ltd, Stroud Gloucestershire

MIX
Paper from
responsible sources
FSC
www.fsc.org   FSC® C004839

Printed and bound in Great Britain by
CPI Antony Rowe, Chippenham, Wiltshire

Contents

Introduction   1

Chapter 1   Making connections   4

Chapter 2   Adapting to radical change   18

Chapter 3   Towards participation   38

Chapter 4   Choosing and using digital technologies   60

Chapter 5   Making, sharing and connecting with digital
             networked technologies   77

Chapter 6   The impact of digital networked technologies on
             teaching and learning   100

Chapter 7   Moving forwards and conclusion   126

Index   145

Introduction

This book is about technology, teaching and learning. Although it considers a number of specific 'technologies' in some detail, it is not a practical guide to these, or a source of technical advice or support. Rather, it is an exploration of the world of technology, pedagogy and practice that you, as a teacher, may want to develop within your work.

The book originated in discussions we had during late 2009. At the time, the 'cross-curricular dimensions' had just been released as part of the new National Curriculum framework. We were particularly interested in the dimension related to technology and agreed to contribute a book focusing on this theme as part of a series to be published touching on each dimension.

However, with the election of a new government in 2010, changes in educational policy and the role of the National Curriculum as a key informant to schools' work led to rethinking about the series. At the time of writing this introduction, we are still awaiting the outcomes of the National Curriculum Review (due in early 2012). However, it seems clear that the 'new' National Curriculum that results from this review process will be slimmer than its predecessor – in both the number of subjects it contains and the amount of content. We are not at all sure that cross-curricularity will be a major theme.

Other political changes have resulted in less focus being placed on technology in education. The abolishment of Becta, the governmental agency that supported the use of information and communication technologies (ICT) in education, has been followed by significant reductions in governmental spending (e.g. halving the amount of money within the Harnessing Technology budget). Time will tell whether the current Coalition Government is an advocate of technology in education.

We mention these curricula and political dimensions to help you understand the broad context for our book. As authors, we believe wholeheartedly that technology has an essential role to play in processes of teaching and learning. Whatever the politicians say, we know that good teachers use a range of technological tools in their classrooms in interesting and creative ways. This will not change.

As educators working within higher education, we do the same. Our experiences here are different. Clive works as a senior lecturer in communication; Jonathan works on courses that prepare students for careers as teachers. However, we are united in this common aim: to help you develop your understanding about, and pedagogy with, technology (whether old or new). We hope to do this by sharing stories from a range of contexts within which teaching and learning take place. Some of these stories will be from the familiar world of the school; others will come from unfamiliar places. We have chosen these deliberately to highlight particular aspects and to challenge conventions and ways of thinking about technology that may be unhelpful.

So, we hope that you are prepared to undertake a journey with us. It starts in the following chapter with an exploration of how technology relates to processes of teaching and learning through a number of case studies drawn from around the world. In Chapter 2, we analyse the impact of digital media within our lives today and the increased flow of information that they facilitate. It reflects on the massive shifts taking place in the ways in which we organise work, do business, look after each other and keep ourselves entertained. Following on from this, we begin to consider what impacts such shifts are having now, and might have in the future, on learning, schools and teaching.

Chapter 3 starts by looking at how the pressures on schools in the United Kingdom to change into participatory learning cultures are being driven by both political and cultural factors. We examine the claim that young people are naturally net savvy. while older generations are always somehow left behind and unable to catch up. We explore some of the evidence about what young people do online and the social skills and understandings they are developing. We will consider what 'literacy' looks like in a digital age and how we might think about it in our own lives and work. Finally, we look at how teachers can support young people in becoming full participants in public and community life.

Chapter 4 is about choices. In particular, it explores the choices you might make about technology and how these choices result in consequences for the processes of teaching and learning. Following on from this consideration of the choices teachers make, we will turn our attention to the choices students make. The chapter will end with an examination of the potential conflicts that can emerge between these two sets of choices, and suggest ways in which this conflict can be resolved.

Making effective choices is central to the construction of an effective pedagogy that uses appropriate tools to facilitate the process of teaching and stimulates learning. However, what you do with the tools you adopt is equally important. Chapter 5 re-examines creativity in the world of social media. It challenges the model of creativity as solely an individual process and looks at how social media can encourage a whole new range of collaborative approaches to education.

These ideas spill over into Chapter 6, where we explore emerging technologies for digital information consumption and production and the impacts they have (or might have) on processes of teaching and learning. We do so by organising those technologies according to the kinds of behaviour they are enhancing: playing, exploring, reflecting and expressing (all key elements of an individual and collaborative creative process). Finally, we show how these technologies can be brought together to form a dynamic learning environment. As we discuss emerging technologies and their use in education, Chapter 6 will also introduce ethical issues and questions for you to think through. We will do that around five areas that we think are under an ethical spotlight as digital networked technologies become ubiquitous.

Our final chapter will bring these key ideas together and attempt to look ahead at possible future education scenarios. It will do this by drawing on ideas from *Beyond Current Horizons*, one of the largest pieces of educational futures research conducted in recent years. Following on from this, we return to your own work as teacher. We will present a series of concluding thoughts about how you might respond to all of this and ensure that you enjoy a sustained, vibrant and fulfilling teaching career.

Each chapter contains a number of practical and reflective tasks. We have written these to help you contextualise some of the key themes of our book within your own teaching. While these are not compulsory, we would encourage you to engage with them and, where possible, use them as part of your broader process of personal and professional development.

As will have become apparent, our journey through the book is wide-ranging. It is not solely about your teaching, your classroom and your school. This is because technology is pervasive. It is not easily contained. We hope that our book will help you consider the broader contexts and ideas that technology facilitates in our culture. In doing so, you will, we hope, be able to recontextualise your teaching alongside sets of ideas and practices. It will be challenging and at times difficult. But it is a journey worth making.

We both work at Manchester Metropolitan University. Jonathan is a Reader in Education and has worked with hundreds of students undertaking courses of initial teacher education, as well as with numerous teachers studying for further degrees.

Collaborating together on this book has been a fascinating journey for both of us. The interchange of ideas from our different backgrounds has led to rewarding discussions and debates. We have both learnt a lot! We trust that, as you engage with this book, this discussion and debate will continue with you, the reader.

To support our book, we have also established an online set of resources. These are organised by chapter (please visit the website at www.routledge. com/9780415620314). You also have the opportunity to contribute to these resources. We would love to hear from you. Do keep in touch and let us know how your journey is going.

Right, it's time to get started ...

1 Making connections

Key questions

- How do your views about technology relate to the broader context of teaching and learning?

- What happens when technology is used to re-imagine the process of teaching and learning?

- Are there links between your development as a teacher and the development of the curriculum, including the role of technology within this?

- What are the key areas for a pedagogy that uses technology that you want to develop?

Many readers of this book will either be starting out, or established, in their careers as teachers. The world of education is tangible and real. It is about knowledge, subjects and their associated cultures, different pedagogical approaches and assessment. It is structured by various curriculum frameworks and examination specifications. It creates a highly ordered system, within which our work is structured within timetables and particular physical spaces. Subjects are domains of, and dominated by, 'experts', and teachers are perceived as 'gatekeepers'. It is a world where we, as teachers, find a sense of identity and community through a common purpose. For many of us, teaching was not a career we chose for money or fame; it was, in the true sense of the word, a vocation (a calling) to which we were drawn.

However, at times, the perceived certainty and solidity of some of these things can be thrown into confusion. Here is a personal reflection of one such time …

April 2011; the hottest April for 350 years. I was standing on Covehithe beach, just south of Southwold on the Suffolk coast, looking out to sea. The blue of the sky merges, seamlessly, into the blue of the water. The horizon is impossible to perceive. Against this backdrop, the shimmering outline of yacht can be seen, impossibly floating against the hazy blue background. For a moment, my eyes played tricks on my mind. Was it floating on water or air? It's hard to tell. It has a ghost-like quality that evades perception and confounds my senses.

Our minds have strange ways of recollecting experiences and making connections. The experience recounted above came to my mind immediately I saw the title Adam Curtis had given to his new series on BBC2 (which began transmission in late May 2011 just before this book's manuscript in its first draft was submitted to our publishers). Curtis named his series *All Watched Over by Machines of Loving Grace* (*Guardian* 2011). This title was not his own. It came from a poem written by Richard Brautigan (in the late 1960s). As you read it, see if you can spot the line that caused me to think of a hot, spring day spent on Covehithe beach:

I like to think (and
the sooner the better!)
of a cybernetic meadow
where mammals and computers
live together in mutually
programming harmony
like pure water
touching clear sky.

I like to think
(right now, please!)
of a cybernetic forest
filled with pines and electronics
where deer stroll peacefully
past computers
as if they were flowers
with spinning blossoms.

I like to think
(it has to be!)
of a cybernetic ecology
where we are free of our labors
and joined back to nature,
returned to our mammal brothers and sisters,

and all watched over
by machines of loving grace.
      (Brautigan 1968)

('… like pure water touching clear sky' – this was the line from the poem that sent my thoughts back a month or so to Suffolk and the 'floating' yacht. But it also made me think in a different way about technology and the role it plays in education.)

Brautigan's poem, *All Watched Over by Machines of Loving Grace*, presents an idyllic, pastoral scene. It can be interpreted in a number of ways. Within the first two stanzas, human beings, animals and technology coexist in mutual harmony within cybernetic meadows and forests. Perhaps Brautigan sees this as an illusion? His stanzas each begin with the phrase 'I like to think', which perhaps indicates a degree of hopefulness. The potential seamlessness of the union between technology and nature is hinted at in the first stanza ('like pure water touching clear sky'). But, as the poem progresses, the gradual realisation of the illusion seems to become apparent (by the third stanza, 'it has to be!'). But this does not prevent the poet from foreseeing, anticipating and hoping for a 'cybernetic ecology where we are free of our labors' and at one with the world.

An alternative reading of the poem could be considerably darker. In this interpretation, perhaps Brautigan's parenthesised comments can be read sarcastically? Technology is perceived as a powerful and increasingly pervasive force coming, by the third stanza, to dominate life and return us to a state of subservience, surveillance and irrelevance, being watched and controlled by 'machines of loving grace'. The contrasts are stark and dark.

Brautigan's poetic eloquence is a sharp contrast to my stumbling metaphor from Covehithe. However, I will pursue it for a little while longer because it speaks of an object (the yacht) positioned, apparently, in two worlds simultaneously (the sea and the sky). Technology is often perceived as other-worldly; we talk of 'virtual worlds' or 'virtual reality' to speak of a new space, one remote from the physical world around us. Some commentators speak of 'augmented reality', which does, by its very terminology, imply an extension beyond our immediate, perceived reality. Brautigan speaks of cybernetic meadows, forests and ecologies; imagined spaces outside our natural world. For all these reasons and many others, it is often understandably easy to divorce technology and its potential impacts from other human activities such as teaching or learning.

So, perhaps our aspiration as teachers is to seek to create that idyllic state where the worlds of education and technology merge, seamlessly, into each other. Like the water and sky in Brautigan's poem, and my experience on Covehithe beach, we might hope that, within this state, it will be impossible to tell where one begins and the other ends. And, within this state, the objects of our attention, the young people whose education we seek to facilitate, will truly be able to move freely. We will help them fly.

But, like Brautigan, our metaphor is an illusion. This seamless technological and educational idyll is unobtainable in the reality of day-to-day life. But it does represent an important metaphor that we would ask you, at the very opening of our book, to consider. The worlds of education and technology are closely, even intimately, related conceptually, philosophically and experientially in the perceived and lived realities of our lives today. Seeking to understand their relationship more fully is essential if we are to function effectively as teachers.

Reflective task

Take a few moments to consider your own view about how technology relates to the processes of teaching and learning. To what extent are these two 'worlds' distinct? In your current teaching, how have you sought to integrate them together and explore any potential points of contact?

We will explore this point further through recounting a story located in a very different part of the world from rural Suffolk – the Kalkaji slum in New Delhi.

Case study 1.1: Holes in the wall

The first computer kiosk was set up in 1999 in the Kalkaji slum in New Delhi, India. For a number of years, Dr Sugata Mitra, then Director of Research at the Centre for Research in Cognitive Systems in India, had been thinking about how computer-based education could serve India's poor. He had a hunch that poor children with little education could teach themselves the basics of computer literacy and, in doing so, open a window to knowledge about the world. To test his idea he embedded a computer with a high-speed Internet connection into a wall (hence, often referred to as 'Hole-in-the-Wall') that divided the institute where he and his team worked from a slum area, strewn with rubbish and used by local street kids. He left the computer on, monitored its use remotely, and installed a video camera in a nearby tree to watch what happened.

What he saw were the ways in which the slum children who hung around in the car park intuitively picked up the skills they needed to use the machine. They self-organised and began teaching themselves what they needed to know with unending curiosity and a thirst for knowledge. The fact that the programs they discovered were all in English was not a problem: they learned the English they needed and even substituted their own words for icons (such as the hourglass that indicates some kind of loading process is taking place) when no words were indicated. Within a few days the children, who were mostly aged 6–10 and who did not attend school, had learned how to browse the Web, play games, create documents and paint pictures. For any parent with children of the same age this would not now appear such a surprising result. Children seem to 'take to' computers in ways that continue to surprise older generations. However, the implications of this social experiment are much more suggestive given its context. This is what Mitra said in an interview in 2000:

> I'm saying that, in situations where we cannot intervene very frequently, you can multiply the effectiveness of 10 teachers by 100- or 1,000-fold if you give children access to the Internet. ... This is a system of education where you assume that children know how to put two and two together on their own. So you stand aside and intervene only if you see them going in a direction that might lead into a blind alley. That's just so that you don't waste time.
>
> (Judge 2000)

This concept of 'minimal intervention' suggests that children can actually teach themselves many of the things that teachers normally assume is their job to teach. Self-directed learning replaces teacher-centric education and frees a teacher's time to support pupils in more individual, personalised ways. The social implications of this are staggering in a world where, despite commitments to universal primary education, some 68 million primary school-age children are currently not enrolled (UNESCO 2011). Mitra's 'Hole-in-the-Wall' is suggestive of the kind of radical transformation that the use of technology could bring to education. That education can improve where there are fewer teachers, not more, is a powerful message. It is not surprising that he was awarded the Best Social Innovation in 2000 by the British Institute for Social Inventions, nor that the ideas behind his experiment have spread. Research into Hole-in-the-Wall computers, now referred to as 'minimally invasive education learning stations', has continued throughout the past ten years and now centres on the ways in which the emergence and development of group social processes aid individual learning. Much of it shows that children learn more through interaction with others, particularly their peers, than in the more passive, receptive activities that dominate formal schooling (Dangwal and Kapur 2009).

In a presentation for TED,[1] Mitra explains how he took the experiment one step further and then exported the idea to the UK. On one trip to a Hole-in-the-Wall computer in India, Mitra asked a young girl to stand behind a group working on the computer and praise what they were doing. He calculated that they achieved 25 per cent more with this positive praise/feedback. The idea of showing off your abilities to an empathetic other, Mitra suggested, was like demonstrating your skills to your Grannie and your Grannie responding, 'That's amazing. I couldn't have done that at your age.'

That insight led to the recruitment of over 200 volunteers in the UK who connect once a week to schools in India via *Skype*. Their task is to encourage and praise the achievements of the youngsters they interact with. It constitutes a coaching and feedback mechanism that integrates with the youngsters' schooling and which is designed to provide a boost to learning. While not all of the volunteers are grandmothers, the initiative is known after its method 'The Granny Cloud'.

Mitra further fine-tuned his experiments in Gateshead, UK, where he worked with 32 children and asked them to work in groups of four using one computer per group. They could change groups, wander between groups and even peer over the shoulder at a group's work and take it back to their group and claim it as theirs. He then gave the groups six GCSE questions to answer. They used everything they could, including *Google*, *Newsgroups*, *Wikipedia* and *Ask Jeeves*. The quickest group answered the questions in 20 minutes and the slowest in 45 minutes. The average score achieved was 76 per cent. The classroom teacher of the groups Mitra was working with was suspicious that what the children had achieved was fingertip knowledge, discovering information that would subsequently be lost. In order to test the hypothesis that no deep learning had taken place during the task, Mitra tested the students with a paper-based exam two months later in which no computers or collaboration were allowed. The average score was 76 per cent.

Reflective task

The two worlds of education and technology collide within this story. What did it tell you about each world, or how the two worlds have come together to produce a new location where learning takes place? What is the role of the teacher within this new space?

Placing the teacher at the heart of curriculum development

Case study 1.1 presents an extreme example of what happened when the 'world' of technology was somewhat forcibly injected into the lives of children within the Kalkaji slum. There are many lessons that one could take from this story. But, for now, we will focus on one key element that is central to this book: the identity and role of the teacher. Mitra's concept of 'minimal intervention' might suggest that the teacher is becoming redundant in the age of digital networked technologies. However, as we will argue throughout this book, nothing could be further from the truth.

Over 50 years ago, the Crowther Report stated that 'everything in education depends ultimately on the teacher' (Central Advisory Council for Education 1959). This viewpoint is encapsulated within the work of one of the greatest educational thinkers of the twentieth century, Lawrence Stenhouse. Stenhouse was a firm advocate for the teacher. It was fitting that the teachers with whom he worked across East Anglia contributed a plaque in his memory. On it, they inscribed Stenhouse's own words: 'It is the teachers who in the end will change the world of the school by understanding it' (Stenhouse 1975: 208).

Stenhouse was well known for his belief that teachers could enhance their professional understanding by engaging in processes of educational research. His notion of the 'teacher as researcher' has done much to shape current thinking about professional development, reflective practice and action research. He was an outspoken critic of what he saw as the deprofessionalisation of the teacher through 'objective-based' curriculum models. For him, such curriculum models were a symbol of distrust of the teacher. He developed alternative ideas that reasserted the teacher's role in curriculum planning and development. If, as he wrote, 'it seems odd to minimise the use of the most expensive resource in the school' (ibid.: 24), it would be better to 'reinvest in the teacher and to construct the curriculum in ways that would enhance teachers' understanding and capability' (Stenhouse 1985: 5).

One of Stenhouse's key beliefs was that there is no curriculum development without teacher development. Developments and changes in education are explicitly tied to the development and changes in the life and work of teachers.

Or, as Skilbeck comments:

> His [Stenhouse's] theory of education is essentially a theory of teacher professionalism, autonomy and development. ... It is the teacher, purposive and free, informed by knowledge and understanding, with clearly articulated values, and a repertoire of practical skills, that he saw as the central agent in the educational enterprise.
>
> (Skilbeck 1983: 12)

These are powerful arguments that apply directly to our discussion of education, technology and the interaction between these two 'worlds'. For, if we adopt a Stenhousian perspective for a moment, it is impossible to imagine any significant educational change empowered through the use of technology without significant, related changes in the lives and working practices of teachers. You have a crucial role to play! While it is common, and perhaps fashionable, to read and hear many proponents of educational technology talk about the contrasts between digital natives (young people) and digital immigrants (teachers), the prioritisation of the learner's voice and the negative contrasts between informal (outside school) and formal (inside school) learning, we are unapologetic in our focus here. The teacher's role is a vital, mediating one that can bring together the worlds of education and technology. This will not happen by accident.

Reflective task

How does the Hole-in-the-Wall computer project and Mitra's concept of 'minimal intervention' fit alongside Stenhouse's mantra of 'no curriculum development without teacher development'? Can you think of parallels to either of these viewpoints (or mixes of them) in your own work as a teacher to this point? (We will consider these ideas again further in Chapter 5.)

Our next case study provides an alternative example of how an individual 'teacher' has begun to exploit technology in interesting ways. Following this chapter's association with different geographical locations, this one has its origins in Davos-Klosters, Switzerland.

Case study 1.2: The Salman Khan Academy

Ever year the Aspen Institute holds an Ideas Festival in which writers, artists, scientists, business leaders, economists and leaders of all kinds meet to listen, discuss, learn and debate critical topics of global import with the aim of making the world a better place. It attracts a great deal of attention and its reputation and influence are similar to those of the annual meeting of the World Economic Forum held in Davos-Klosters.

In 2010 Bill Gates appeared at the Ideas Festival and, in an interview with Walter Isaacson, the President of the Aspen Institute, began to lament the unsustainable, spiralling costs of education in the United States of America. As an antidote to the current crisis, Gates talked at length about Salman Khan, a former hedge-fund manager who now dedicates his time to producing educational resources, which Gates's 11-year-old son had been using for the past few months. Gates senior was full of admiration for the 10–15-minute tutorials that his son had been watching on topics ranging from algebra to biology. 'Unbelievable', he called them, which, from someone with as much influence and reach as Bill Gates, was significant praise and a remark-able endorsement. It was probably not unexpected from Khan himself, however, whose website *The Khan Academy* had won the Microsoft Tech Award for Education in 2009. That award was given in recogni-tion of Khan's exceptional ability to teach complicated concepts in ways that are easy to understand, and to do so at zero cost and in a way that everyone could access.

The story of the Khan Academy begins in 2004 when he was asked to help a family member who lived in another city improve their maths score at school. The 'lessons' were initially given over the phone but, because of different time zones (Salman lived in Boston and his cousin in New Orleans) and busy schedules, he began to upload short video classes to *YouTube*, which his cousin (and a growing group of friends) could watch on their computers. Initially sceptical that without the dialogue they had on the telephone his cousins would quickly lose interest, he was soon reassured that the loss of interac-tion (*'Are you sure you understand? So what is the answer to …?'*) was easily compensated for by the fact that they could watch the videos when they wanted and however many times they wanted in order to understand the lesson. They could also build up a library of lessons that they could revisit whenever they wanted and avoid the embarrassment of having forgotten something that had been explained to them weeks before.

So Khan carried on making his tutorials. He was clearly well qualified to do so. With three Bachelor's degrees (in mathematics, computer science and electrical engineering) from MIT and an MBA from Harvard, he feels confident to give talks on subjects ranging from basic maths to history. With his videos on *YouTube*, Khan's virtual pupils were spreading beyond family members and their friends and he began to receive emails from around the world complimenting him on his classes and how they had helped improve their viewers' understanding and results in school tests. He gave up his job in May 2009 to continue to expand his venture in order to help more people learn more. His motivation is not financial. With donations from Microsoft and Google, Khan is able to pay himself a salary, but his overriding goal is to make the Academy a sustainable not-for-profit organisation within the next five years. He writes on the website's FAQ:

> When I'm 80, I want to feel that I helped give access to a world-class education to billions of students around the world. Sounds a lot better than starting a business that educates some subset of the developed world that can pay $19.95/month and eventually selling it to some text book company or something.
>
> (Khan 2011)

As of February 2011 there were more than 2,000 video lessons available, making the Academy the largest virtual school in the world. Multilingual translations and video subtitling by an army of volunteers are enabling more people to learn from them.

Khan's ideas are radical. His pedagogy takes as its starting point the notion encapsulated by Coleman Hawkins, the jazz saxophonist, who is famously quoted as saying: 'If you don't make mistakes, you aren't really trying.' Mastery, in this view, comes from failure and experimentation, not from rewarding test-taking ability and penalising failure. Equally, when mastery is the objective, a structured curriculum that standardises learning in lockstep is an anathema. That does not mean that Khan's lessons are not relevant to national standards. When mastery is achieved it can be expressed and incorporated into any curriculum.

Khan abandoned one type of interaction and feedback when he stopped using the telephone to tutor his cousins remotely. In the Academy he has replaced it with data monitoring and analysis. For example, *YouTube* provides data showing if, and at which point, viewers get distracted and abandon a particular lesson. This allows Khan to review such points and ask himself how they might be improved to increase attention. The site monitors how users who register with the site use the materials. The resulting 'Detailed Performance Metrics' have a high level of granularity, meaning that very focused, elaborate data are collected, which enables specific feedback to encourage progress. This adaptive model, where the machine constantly responds to individuals' learning needs and provides tailored support and instruction on the basis of those needs, is at the heart of the Khan Academy and its plans for the future.

What Khan has put together is an infrastructure for the delivery of online content. He is explicit about his pedagogy and his approach to curriculum. On the Academy website Khan talks about more than 2,000 different topics. But he is in no way precious about his, or anybody else's, 'method'. On the contrary, he encourages the use of his lessons, the analytics and targeted feedback that are incorporated into his software, by any school that wishes to use them. But, while not against schools per se, Khan's Academy and its success are a critique of current organised schooling constructed around bricks and mortar and running a 9.00 to 3.30 structured regime.

In some ways, the genesis of this book also reflects this key assertion that there is no curriculum development without teacher development. Originally, it was due to be part of a series of books designed to help teachers adopt 'cross-curricular dimensions' within their teaching. Cross-curricular dimensions were part of the National Curriculum for Key Stage 3 that was introduced in 2008. Having established a personal link as authors for this title, we began to plan a book towards this end.

However, recent political changes resulted in this, and many other curriculum frameworks, being either dropped completely or significantly reviewed. As such, we thought it inappropriate to write a book about a defunct curriculum structure.

Reflective task

Case study 1.2 presents an interesting account of one teacher's development of new forms of educational content inspired or mediated by pieces of technology. Think through the following questions:

- What are the key elements of this teacher's pedagogy and how did they emerge as he responded to the adoption of new pieces of technology within his educational provision?

- What evidence does this story provide of Stenhouse's assertion that there is 'no curriculum development without teacher development'?

- In a world where educational content is available on demand, where and how can schools and teachers 'add value' to the educational process?

But, by this time, our work as two academics and authors was beginning to interrelate in interesting ways. While one of us has experience of working as a teacher in schools and in delivering courses of initial teacher education within an Institute of Education, the other works as a lecturer in communication and new media within a Faculty of Health, Psychology and Social Care. In many ways, our working lives are very different. Yet we have common interests and, having worked together on this book for the last 18 months or so, we would say that our own work and teaching have been enriched and developed through a process of collaborative research, analysis and structured reflection that we needed to engage with in order to write a book like this.

Summary

This opening chapter started with the assertion that the worlds of technology and education are inextricably linked. Within formal schooling, teachers play a vital role. While other factors such as curriculum and qualification frameworks have important roles to play, we believe that the identity and skilful pedagogy of individual teachers are central to the provision of quality approaches to teaching that result in engaging opportunities for young people's learning. Therefore, it is essential that teachers fully understand the potential affordances and limitations of technology in the educational process. To do this, it is crucial that all teachers have a broader understanding of technology as a social and cultural force, as well as an understanding of how it relates to the educational processes of teaching and learning.

Discussion points

- How do the broader societal and cultural forces that shape technology and its use impact on processes of teaching and learning? What examples can you give from your own experience?

- Are the worlds of technology and education inextricably linked? How would your pupils respond to this idea? Are there examples of them learning informally with technology that you could draw on to help develop your own pedagogy?

- Consider an activity or area of knowledge where you have achieved a level of mastery. To what extent was that mastery achieved by failure and experimentation? How has your teaching been influenced as a result?

Useful websites/resources

www.hole-in-the-wall.com/   Hole-in-the-Wall learning methodology
www.khanacademy.org/   Khan Academy

Note

1   www.ted.com/talks/lang/eng/sugata_mitra_the_child_driven_education.html.

References

Brautigan, R. (1968) *The Pill Versus the Springhill Mine Disaster*, New York: Dell.
Central Advisory Council for Education (1959) *Crowther Report*, London: HMSO.
Dangwal, R. and Kapur, P. (2009) 'Learning through teaching: peer-mediated instruction in minimally invasive education', *British Journal of Educational Technology*, 40: 5–22.
Guardian (2011) 'All watched over by machines of loving grace'. Available online: www.guardian.co.uk/culture/video/2011/may/06/documentary-internet-adam-curtis (accessed 9 May 2011).
Judge, P. (2000) 'An interview with Sugata Mitra: a lesson in computer literacy from India's poorest kids', *Bloomberg Business Week*. Available online: www.businessweek.com/bwdaily/dnflash/mar2000/nf00302b.htm (accessed 9 May 2011).

Khan, S. (2011) 'About Khan Academy'. Available online: www.khanacademy.org/about/faq (accessed 9 May 2011).

Skilbeck, M. (1983) 'Lawrence Stenhouse: research methodology, *British Educational Research Journal*, 9: 11–20.

Stenhouse, L. (1975) *An Introduction to Curriculum Research and Development*, London: Heinemann.

Stenhouse, L. (1985) 'Product or process? A reply to Brian Crittenden', in Ruddock, J. and Hopkins, D. (eds) *Research as a Basis for Teaching*, London: Heinemann Education.

UNESCO (2011) *The Hidden Crisis: Armed conflict and education*, Paris: UNESCO.

2

Adapting to radical change

Key questions

- How is technology changing the way we think, live and work?
- How can we begin to respond to these changes in the ways in which we teach?
- In a world where knowledge and information are a few clicks away, is there going to be a role for the teacher for much longer? If yes, what will that teacher actually be doing?

Introduction

The world is changing. There are approximately two billion Internet and five billion mobile phone connections worldwide. Life without digital technologies, and in particular digital media, would not be life as we now know it. As information is increasingly digitised and communication becomes embedded in digital networks, massive shifts are taking place in the ways in which we organise work, do business, look after each other and keep ourselves entertained. The ways we learn are changing and the ways we teach are beginning to respond to those changes. In this chapter we reflect on some of the most significant trends emerging in this complex landscape, including:

- the emergence of a new way of sharing knowledge;
- changes in the ways we get things done;
- the acceleration of how knowledge and information are shared;
- the way we connect to people, including our pupils.

Also, we begin to consider what impacts these trends are having now, and might have in the future, on learning, schools and teaching.

We are starting this chapter with two stories. The first looks at the different working routines of two writers, J. G. Ballard and Cory Doctorow. Their writing lives overlapped (Ballard produced his last novel in 2006 and Doctorow his first in 2003), but the ways in which they worked illustrate some of the changes to writing, publishing and sharing information. The second story shows how new digital tools and networks are enabling people with no previous experience (in this story, Leslie Allison) to dabble and play with media, find audiences and inspire others to do the same.

Reflective task

These two stories are not directly about schools or teachers. This is a deliberate choice on our part. We have included them as a challenge to our thinking as educators. As you read them, reflect on the changes that they illustrate. Are similar changes taking place in education? Consider the following questions.

- Are we, as the producers and distributors of knowledge, facing a similar future?
- What might be the consequences and even the opportunities?
- Does the world of the dabbler have a counterpart in the world of education?

Case study 2.1: Ballard and Doctorow

In a 1984 interview published in the *Paris Review*, J. G. Ballard, the dystopian novelist of, most famously, *The Empire of the Sun* and *Crash*, describes his daily working habits:

Every day, five days a week. Longhand now, it's less tiring than a typewriter. When I'm writing a novel or a story I set myself a target of about seven hundred words a day, sometimes a little more. I do a first draft in longhand, then do a very careful longhand revision of the text, then type out the final manuscript. I used to type first and revise in longhand, but I find that modern fiber-tip pens are less effort than a typewriter. Perhaps I ought to try a seventeenth century quill. I re-write a great deal, so the word processor sounds like a dream. My neighbour is a BBC videotape editor and he offered to lend me his, but apart from the eye-aching glimmer, I found that the editing functions are terribly laborious.

(Frick 1984)

If Ballard is describing a lost world, there is little change to it 20 years later when, in conversation with Simon Sellers, he describes how set in his ways he had become:

I don't have a PC. I'm not on the Internet and I think that's a matter of age. I'm nearly 76 now and I think the personal computer and the Internet really came in about 10 years ago. And by then I was an old dog and the Internet was a new trick. I mean, I still write my novels in longhand and type them out on an old electric typewriter. I don't have any modern appliances.

(Sellers 2006)

Ballard's habits and rituals reflect those of many twentieth-century novelists and writers. The production of his writing was shaped by the tools he used. The consumption of his novels by his readers was similarly shaped by the processes that structured the industry that printed and distributed his work.

Cory Doctorow, like Ballard an author of speculative fiction, has similar habits and rituals to Ballard:

When I'm working on a story or novel, I set a modest daily goal – usually a page or two – and then I meet it every day, doing nothing else while I'm working on it. It's not plausible or desirable to try to get the world to go away for hours at a time, but it's entirely possible to make it all shut up for 20 minutes. Writing a page every day gets me more than a novel per year – do the math – and there's always 20 minutes to be found in a day, no matter what else is going on.

(Doctorow 2009)

But his tools are different. Unlike Ballard, he uses computers to write and insists that the worst piece of advice he ever received was to keep away from the Internet while he was writing because it would waste his time and distract him from the task at hand. Doctorow is a prolific writer. He writes at least a novel a year, novellas and short stories, countless journalism pieces, daily blog posts and speeches for his digital activism work.

Doctorow's recent book, *With a Little Help*, was released simultaneously in bookshops and online as a freely shareable ebook. It is a collection of reprints of stories previously published in various magazines. The title is apt. Friends with skills in sound production and broadcast reading, computer geeks with the ability to hack technical solutions to file formats, and cover designers have all contributed to its development. Tools such as *Twitter* and *Flickr* have been used to solve problems and quiz the likely readers of the work.

Unsure how to pack the book for shipping, Doctorow came upon the idea of using burlap coffee sacks. He wondered whether it would work. He took a picture of a prototype, uploaded it to the photo-sharing site *Flickr* and asked his *Twitter* followers if they would like to receive the book packaged as in the photograph. The overwhelming response was positive, with tweets advising on the use of acid-free paper between the book and the burlap and others providing URLs for where such sacking could be bought.

Case study 2.2: Leslie Allison and *Xtranormal*

Like many aspiring academics in the United States of America, Leslie Allison felt frustrated at the diminishing opportunities for full-time, tenured teaching and research that would give job security and intellectual freedom. After watching a video parodying the admissions interview for an American Law School, she thought she could spoof her own journey towards academia in the same style. Using *Xtranormal*,[1] a cartoon-to-video website, she spent 90 minutes creating a four-and-a-half-minute animation called *So You Want to Get a PhD in the Humanities*, which she then uploaded to *Facebook* and

YouTube.[2] Within three months almost a million viewers had chuckled their way through the caustic satire between the graduate student and her cynical supervisor. Her video joined countless others made with *Xtranormal*, which, under the rubric '*So You Want to …*', satirise the naive expectations of people whose ambitions are 'simply' to become a librarian or to close a *Facebook* account.

Allison is an aspiring academic and not an aspiring film maker. As a student of literature she felt that an appropriate form for expressing her ideas would be a satirical animation. An article in the local or academic newspaper may not have attracted the audience she had in mind and, like a personal blog post, would have been difficult to write in a way that would have avoided her being accused of narcissistic ranting. When she read *Xtranormal*'s promise, 'If you can type, you can make a movie', she playfully gave it a try. It was very simple. Pre-designed characters offered on the site are made to speak by typing a script. The synthetic voices that speak the script sound robotic, although curiously that adds to the appeal of the overall film. The editing was simple and the uploading to *Facebook* and *YouTube* seamless. Leslie was proof that, as Chief Executive of *Xtranormal*, Graham Sharp, said, 'Historically there's been no way of anyone making a movie this easily … we've become the tool that every niche group can make videos with.'[3]

After trying to sell the system to professional animators, *Xtranormal* realised that it would be the dabblers, those consumers who wanted to have a go at making animation films, who would be its main customers. With so many young academics looking at the '*So You Want to …*' sub-genre, it was unsurprising that the idea of using the tools in an instructional way emerged in the comments both on *YouTube* and *Facebook*, but also on *Xtranormal*'s site itself where movies can also be stored. As the company monitored this interest, they realised that there was a market for using quickly produced animation films in the classroom. The sub-genre '*So You Want to …*' very easily adapts into the instructional video '*How to …*'.

Technology and a new form of production

Ballard worked in a world of publishers and printing presses. For our purposes here, however, one simple though far-reaching idea is worth emphasising: the printing press, as a type of technology, revolutionised the way we read and publish and, in so doing, created a sharp division between readers and writers. This was because printing was expensive and access controlled by elites with the wealth and power to own them. There was a massive increase in the number of readers, but the number of published writers was always far, far fewer. Even our understanding of what it means to be 'a writer' ('someone who has been published by a publisher'?) is indebted to this gatekeeping role performed by those who control the printing presses.

With the Internet a new model is emerging that allows every reader potentially to become a writer. We no longer need expensive printing presses and complex distribution chains, or book proposals for publishers. Those barriers have now been removed. Instead, a computer connected to the Internet *is* a printing press and a channel to a potential audience of all those similarly connected. Cory Doctorow's story illustrates this paradigm shift. He is able to sideline his publisher. He overturns traditional copyright. He adds ebooks. His readers join him as writers (in truth, editors, but the principle is important) and production assistants in informal collaboration. He is able to control his own cottage industry in a way that was unthinkable even ten years ago.

Leslie Allison's experiences are equally instructive of this paradigm change. Broadcast television, in many ways, has been an extension of the invention of the printing press: expensive production processes controlled by small elites who broadcast content to a mass audience. The possibilities of creating content and broadcasting it in that world of mass media (whether television or radio) were equally controlled by gatekeepers keen to limit entry to a vetted, chosen few. If the computer gave Doctorow a printing press, it has given Allison a video-production suite and broadcast capabilities.

Many commentators across a variety of disciplines have been trying to make sense of this paradigm shift. Technology is creating a 'bottom-up' approach to production. Industries that are traditionally hierarchical, and where professional security is most entrenched, are particularly vulnerable. In *Here Comes Everybody*, Clay Shirky explains how.

He starts by looking at the idea of a 'profession':

> Most professions exist because there is a scarce resource that requires ongoing management: librarians are responsible for organising books on the shelf, newspaper executives are responsible for deciding what goes on the front page.
> (Shirky 2008: 57)

Scarcity creates the need for the professional. The profession is, in part, an in-group with entry requirements and behavioural norms. Once 'in', those behavioural norms ('professional conduct') begin to colour the very way you see the world. Being a 'teacher' colours your understanding of the world around you.

This rather insular, inward-looking nature of a profession is one of its strengths: it maintains quality and monitors performance. But, according to Shirky, it is also its biggest weakness:

> In any profession, particularly one that has existed long enough that no one can remember a time when it didn't exist, members have a tendency to equate provisional solutions to particular problems with deep truths about the world.
>
> (ibid.: 59)

The idea that publishers should publish books and film companies produce films has become an ingrained, naturalised belief. But it was also a provisional solution to the particular problem of scarcity. When anybody can publish anything at almost zero cost, that scarcity goes away and the belief falls apart. That is why the publishing and audio–visual industries are now questioning some of their more ingrained working practices in order to survive.

Should teachers feel threatened by this trend? What are the potential consequences? For example, is the belief that we should only be taught by certified teachers in certified institutions simply a provisional solution based on a particular scarcity (those with the requisite skills and knowledge), a scarcity which is now beginning to disappear?

Reflective task

Our two case studies from the world of publishing and content creation have examined the ways in which a new publishing paradigm is changing the ways in which information is produced and consumed. This is disrupting some of the more ingrained beliefs of media professions and professionals. Teaching is not a media profession nor, as someone reading this book, are you likely to be working for a traditional media company. However, we believe that these changes will have an impact on education, on our beliefs about the nature of schools, and on teaching and learning. So, for example, how would you respond to the following questions?

- If Cory Doctorow were a teacher in school, how do you think he would be producing materials for his pupils?
- If Cory Doctorow was a pupil in your school, how would you be seeking to encourage, develop and reward his particular approach to writing?
- What are some of the future roles for teachers in Leslie Allison's world of do-it-yourself media culture?

Technology and a new form of education

Digital networked technologies are now allowing people to do things without needing those institutions that traditionally acted as gatekeepers. The two case studies that follow have been included to give you a taste of some of the ways in which individuals are finding opportunities to learn through digital networked technologies. As we get closer to a world of learning, think of parallels in your own lives where what you do and how you do it are radically altered by the use of these technologies.

Case study 2.3: Tom and his guitar

Tom, my 14-year-old nephew, was desperate to learn the guitar. My brother suggested a teacher, someone who would come around to the house once a week. Tom was excited, his enthusiasm contagious and a week later a young guitar teacher appeared at the door. The lessons lasted four weeks. Tom became bored, practised less and less, said he did not like the teacher or the music he wanted him to play and most definitely wanted to bow out of the arrangement. His Dad was resigned to this being another one of those avenues that led to a bit of a cul-de-sac, at least for the moment. He was sure Tom would find another to explore soon enough.

Six months later and, as I walked into my brother's house for a visit, I heard music coming from Tom's room. Good music. A guitar band with passable soloing and a steady groove. I wondered who it was. My brother told me to wander in. I found Tom plugged into his laptop, moving his eyes between a *YouTube* video and his guitar fret board. He had set up a system where he could slow down guitar parts to learn them more easily, he had accompanying drum and bass patterns to help him keep time, and he uploaded his practice sessions so that a group of his friends, having similar musical adventures, could hear what he was doing and leave comments. It was serious fun. Instead of one teacher a week coming round to the kitchen table, Tom was learning what he needed to know from *YouTube* videos and guitar forums.

Two months later and one of Tom's friends introduced him to *ccMixter*.[4] Now he began uploading his musical sketches and even complete songs. The other members on the site were able to download

Tom's music, see what he had been doing in the online sequencer, overdub their own guitar parts, remix the song and share the result with the group. This remixing was infectious and multiple versions of Tom's songs began appearing. Perhaps the most important part of this, though, was the 'liking' system where Tom would receive 'likes' of his songs and comments left by other musicians. These were not his friends from school but musicians from all over the world. He was initially worried about being criticised for his offerings. However, he quickly noticed that there was an unwritten convention: 'No "slagging off"; when you come across something good, say that it is good.'

A musician who was remixing and overdubbing Tom's music more than any other suggested that they get together online to 'jam'. They both looked around at various sites where they would be able to play together over the Internet in real time. They found *jamLink*,[5] which allowed them to play, record, edit and mix their music. They uploaded the finished results to *ccMixter* where, once again, the community commented, downloaded, remixed and overdubbed.

Tom learned a whole host of different things in that time and with those tools – not least, how to learn from others and play with others.

Case study 2.4: The bike

I have always had a fascination with bikes, particularly older bikes. When my wife said she wanted to start cycling again and definitely did not want a mountain bike, I suggested she looked for an older 'ladies' bike' – one of those elegant, classic bicycles with wicker baskets, that I could clean up. After scouring the local papers and second-hand bike shops she eventually found just what she was looking for at a reclamation yard. However, more than needing just a clean-up, this old bike was in pretty poor condition and looked like it needed a complete overhaul.

I was curious as to exactly what it was. I scoured the cycle shops online and searched various manufacturers but emerged none the wiser. I had been using the photo-sharing site *Flickr* for a couple of years, uploading holiday pictures to share with family and friends. I uploaded several photos of the rusted classic and added them to a group pool called 'Vintage Bicycles' with a common title of 'Can anyone identify this?' Within three hours I had ten replies on a dedicated discussion forum for the group. It was definitely an original Raleigh Ladies' 21-inch, 3-speed Roadster with a Brooks B66 saddle built in the 1940s. I even compared it to other photos tagged with those keywords in the group pool. So began two months of amateur restoration, during which time I was a regular visitor to the *Flickr* group, uploading works-in-progress, discussing various processes of dismantling and reassembling obscure parts, discovering specialist suppliers of vintage components, cleaning and repainting. This was like an online workshop with people at different levels of ability and stages of restoration helping each other out, absorbing new information and new skills and passing those on to any novices as they arrived.

With the bike now cleaned, reassembled and 'fairly' roadworthy, I was left with a final job for which pictures and written descriptions were leaving me less than confident. Sturmey Archer is a company renowned for producing bicycle hub gears. Unlike modern gear manufacturers, this company builds its gears inside the rear-wheel hub, tidily hidden from view. These internal gears are not only difficult to access but, to eyes as unaccustomed as mine to complex machinery and precision engineering, appear daunting to overhaul. Poring over online manuals, detailed descriptions and photographs of the various components that I was pointed to failed to build my confidence. I really did not think I could take this hub apart, remove and replace the component that I knew was broken, and reassemble the whole thing in a way that would ensure the functioning of three gears at the press of a simple lever on the handlebars.

I needed help – someone to show me, hands-on, how it was done. Again, I was pointed in the right direction. GrahamNR17 had recently uploaded a 9-minute video showing how to strip and rebuild exactly the same hub as the one I was struggling with. I absorbed the video through multiple viewings and, growing in confidence, began the work accompanied by GrahamNR7 on the laptop in the shed. Through 'play and pause' (just like Tom's guitar teachers, this instructor repeated everything I needed to hear as many times as I needed to hear it), I worked my way slowly but surely through the stages and, with a sigh of relief, remounted the rear wheel, connected the gear cable and was able to change from first through to third and back again. I was triumphant. The bike was finished.

New ways of doing things

In many ways these stories are unremarkable. There are hundreds of thousands of young teens like Tom and thousands of middle-aged men like myself. With three-quarters of UK households now connected to the Internet, *YouTube* reaching 17.5 million monthly users in May 2010 and a quarter of 16–24-year-olds claiming to have made a short video and uploaded it to a website (Ofcom 2010: 165), such activities are no longer the exclusive domain of the 'geek'. While communicating, authoring and sharing may be more popular among younger users, there is a general growth in such activities across those now using the Internet. Uploading photos to a website was the most popular form of content creation in the UK across all age groups in 2010 (ibid.: 271).

However, what is remarkable about our stories is the new ways of learning that they illustrate. This form of learning takes place outside institutions, without teachers and without timetables. It is not what Tom and I learned, but *how* we learned, that is most significant here.

It seems that Tom's motivation to learn was not fully appreciated by the teacher who visited his house. Guitar playing was perhaps more closely linked to his developing sense of identity than to a love of solfège and the precise fingerings of particular scales. Tom learned what he needed to when he needed to. There were parameters ('computer time', meals, etc.) but his 'recording studio' never closed and it was an almost unlimited information source. Nor did the tuition that he used ever get bored in repeating the same instructions or showing him the same chord progressions; he simply replayed until he had mastered the point. He was in control of his own learning. However, more important than this was the opportunity that Tom and myself had to join larger learning communities. With time, experience and practice we both became fluent in those communities.

Perhaps the most significant learning that Tom experienced took place in the comments, exchanges and remixes that he engaged in with his peer group. Some might think that such interaction online was cold and isolating. In fact, when Tom was with a teacher in the kitchen working his way through Ex. 6 from Book 1, he was more isolated than when he was involved in a social and cultural process online. The opportunity to participate, collaborate and interact enabled and deepened his learning through play, practice and experimentation, which often led to unplanned and innovative discoveries. It allowed the more experienced to help the less, and for sub-groups to develop organically from shared interests. So, Tom began jamming with another musician and then uploaded the results so that the wider community could comment.

These stories show us how new media technologies favour the amateur (the word comes from Latin, where it originally meant 'lover of') and create the spaces where such amateurs can participate and learn. When content is produced in a networked, participatory environment, the boundaries between producers and consumers break down. Production, as understood in a conventional, industrial sense, gives way to new processes in which relationships between producers and consumers, facilitated by a networked environment, lead to the emergence of what Charles Leadbeater calls 'pro/am' – a blend of professional and amateur (Leadbeater and Miller 2004); Axel Bruns calls 'produsage' – another blend, this time of production and usage (Bruns 2008); and Clay Shirky refers to as 'mass amateurization' (Shirky 2008). All of these writers agree that new communication capabilities are creating the conditions for radically new ways in which information can be produced and consumed – they just can't agree on exactly what to call it. The spaces afforded by such capabilities are, as James Gee argues, 'affinity spaces' (Gee 2004: 70) – spaces where barriers (such as age, educational level and socio-economic level) to participation are levelled, and where, if you have a shared interest and motivation, you can express yourself, learn and teach.

Reflective task

- What have you communicated, authored and shared in this new digital world? How did you learn to do so?

- If it is true that most young people seem to pick up their skills in using those digital technologies we have been looking at, do we need to teach them? Or do people do better when they are simply left to experiment and adapt?

- If you do think they could be taught, what links do you think could be made between the school curriculum and such skills?

Technology, openness and ownership

There was a time in the early 1980s when I felt my authority as a teacher was, in part, based on my exclusive access to the materials I taught to my students. I had the books, the lecture notes and the acetates for the overhead projector. As I began teaching, I divulged the stock of knowledge I had carried with me down the long corridor and into the classroom. When the class finished, that stock was tidied up and returned to its filing cabinet in the office at the other end of the corridor. As the sole owner of the source, my job was to bestow it on a group of students whose task was to digest it before it was once again hidden from view.

This was a proprietary model based on the control and ownership of the materials considered relevant to the curriculum. It gave me confidence to have those materials, the content needed to teach the course, safely hidden away. Given how labour-intensive the process of producing those resources was, it is unsurprising how possessive I became of them. Before the photocopier, the only inexpensive way of producing multiple copies for classroom study, homework or tests was to type the text on to waxed paper stencils (using a manual typewriter with the ribbon removed), which were then attached to a mimeograph machine. The machine was hand-cranked and paper fed between the drum and the pressure roller. As the drum turned, ink was squeezed through the holes in the paper made by the ribbon-less typewriter and the copies emerged. Needless to say, there was no last-minute copying!

It was only between a small circle of colleagues that materials were shared. There was an institutional repository of stencils that could be run through the mimeograph, but these were limited to common institutional materials such as course descriptions and exams. Teaching materials, it was generally acknowledged, were as personal as the books on your bookshelves or records in a record collection.

This all changed with the introduction of digital technologies and digital networks. Digital technologies turned those card-backed wax stencils into zeroes and ones. Words no longer needed to be printed on paper, but instead could be printed on screen and distributed on floppy disks. Once information goods are freed from their physical form they are also freed from the law of diminishing returns (Carr 2008). In the pre-digital world of mimeographs, my pain of producing more to satisfy the desire to share was simply too much; the gain was not worth the pain. By the mid-1980s, digital networks led to a local area network distributing resources without the need for floppy disks. Study texts, homework and exams were being sent from a server to individual computers in a computer 'lab', where students could complete and store them for further, individual use. These were exhilarating times (and this was still before the advent of the World Wide Web) in which the magic of shared resources was matched by the seeming naturalness of computers to share such resources.

Moving to the present day, wikis provide a powerful example of this kind of sharing and openness. A wiki is simply a website that any visitor can contribute to or edit. The largest wiki, of course, is *Wikipedia*. The English version of *Wikipedia* has 3.2 million articles, 25 times as many articles as the next largest English-language encyclopedia, the *Encyclopaedia Britannica*.[6]

Wikipedia has a trusted core of 2,000 volunteer administrators who edit, monitor and protect the site from digital vandals. The Wikimedia Foundation oversees the technical aspects of keeping *Wikipedia*'s web servers running, which, with the number of visitors and the quantity of information stored, is no mean feat. However, with only 50 full-time employees, it is the work of thousands of people who donate their time, expertise and financial support that keeps the initiative alive and free of advertising.

Apart from these staggering statistics and innovative organisation, it is the idea that *Wikipedia* has displaced a 200-year-old institution, the *Encyclopaedia Britannica*, that has been of most cultural significance in the last ten years. This open structure, to which visitors do not need passwords or membership to access the content, nor certificated knowledge to make a contribution, now receives a staggering one out of every 200 page views on the Web.[7] *Wikipedia* is now used as a press source,[8] cited in academic work[9] and used in legal proceedings in courts.[10]

If *Wikipedia* is used as an authoritative source in these contexts, why are educators seemingly so reluctant to use it with their students, at times warned off it,[11] or even banned from accepting it from students as a source in written assignments?[12] The arguments tend to centre on questions of authority, accuracy and appropriateness.

In a 2005 study for the journal *Nature*, the accuracy of the science entries in *Wikipedia* was compared with those in the *Encyclopaedia Britannica*. 'The exercise revealed numerous errors in both encyclopaedias, but among 42 entries tested, the difference in accuracy was not particularly great: the average science entry in *Wikipedia* contained around four inaccuracies; *Britannica*, about three' (Giles 2005: 900). There are two significant points here. The first is that Giles's study shows that neither encyclopaedia gets it right all of the time. There are factual errors in both and both include information that is outdated. The idea that an encyclopaedia is an authority whose accuracy transcends time is simply wrong. Countries change their geographical borders. Planets are redefined. A print publication has to struggle to keep up with such changes. Much of our knowledge is contentious. It emerges from a process of hypothesis, debate, evidence, debate and further hypothesis. Such a process is largely oblique in the *Encyclopaedia Britannica*.

In *Wikipedia*, instead, it is central to the emergence of a current piece of knowledge. The history of discussion and debate, of edits and alterations, is recorded and visible. Not only is it visible, we are invited to contribute to the process, not on the basis of any predefined authority or credibility that we may have from other contexts, but on the basis of what we can offer to the state of current knowledge. That is a new authority and relationship to authority that we have been endowed with. It is an authority that emerges from the process and an architecture that has built into it transparency and openness to scrutiny. It is most definitely not an authority that comes from recognised 'expert' knowledge. Some 40 per cent of the edits that take place on *Wikipedia* are made by anonymous contributors. This is an interesting cultural change. Expert knowledge, the kind of knowledge that has been the currency of schools and academic institutions, has to be earned in *Wikipedia*. It is not a pre-given on the basis of reputation.

If *Wikipedia* has replaced the *Encyclopaedia Britannica* as a first stop for current knowledge, its ethos has been influential in a far wider arena. *Wikileaks*,[13] which emerged in 2001, is mounting what is perhaps the largest-scale challenge to such opacity we have yet witnessed. A non-profit media organisation, *Wikileaks* makes it possible for independent sources to leak information anonymously on to its website. When, in 2010, *Wikileaks* posted 75,000 military logs, 400,000 documents charting the war in Iraq and a few thousand of the quarter of a million confidential diplomatic cables it had received, an information war began. It is a war between 'the naturally open systems of the present and the closed system of the past' (Sifrey 2011: 38). It is also part of a long-term trend that favours more transparency and more openness in all sectors of public life. These are new challenges to authority, whether educational, scientific or political, which are having significant impacts on public services and public servants. Education is not immune.

Practical task

Read the article 'Wikipedia: neutral point of view',[14] which describes *Wikipedia*'s editing policy, then choose any article from *Wikipedia* and ask yourself whether the policy has been adhered to and, if so, how.

- What parallels do you see between 'Neutral point of view' and your own teaching practice in presenting 'contentious' topics?
- How could you use *Wikipedia*'s policy as a way of mediating classroom discussion?

The ubiquity of information

'Never before in the history of the planet have so many people – on their own – had the ability to find so much information about so many things and about so many other people' (Friedman 2007: 177).

In 2003, two economists at the University of California, Berkeley, Hal Varian and Peter Lyman, calculated the total global information production for one year. They included information on all analogue media such as paper, film and tape, as well as digital media such as hard disks and microchips, and all TV, radio and telecommunications. The total they came up with for the year 2000 reached 1.5 exabytes, which they explain is equivalent to 37,000 times the complete print collection held in the US Library of Congress. That was just the information for one year. Within three years they calculated that it had doubled. The volume of information on the Web in 2002 was 17,000 times the size of the US Library of Congress (Lyman et al. 2003). A more recent study (Hilbert and Lopez 2011) suggests that we can now store more than 295 exabytes of information in analogue and digital form, which equals 15 times the size of an average university library per person, and doubles every three or four years. Our capacity to broadcast information is also accelerating. According to the same report, we each receive 2 zettabytes of information by broadcast technology, which corresponds to 175 newspapers per person, while the amount that we each communicate bidirectionally amounts to six newspapers per day. However, the fastest rate of growth is in computational power, which is still doubling every 18 months, as Moore's Law suggested it would. That growth suggests that the trend for this phenomenal growth in information is likely to continue and, if anything, increase. It is hard to appreciate. Jaron Lanier tries an image: 'It's as if you kneel to plant the seed of a tree and it grows so fast that it swallows your whole town before you can even rise to your feet' (2010: 8).

We cannot possibly keep up with the information that is broadcast to us through the various channels that are now available. As teachers, we will need strategies to cope (and these will be explored in Chapter 6). But if we think of information as just being something that we consume, then, ultimately, given the trends described above, we can only ever drown. However, this information-centric view is limiting and distorting, particularly in the field of education, when we want to take full advantage of new technologies to enable people to become better thinkers and learners. Fortunately, there is another way to think about information.

In *The Social Life of Information*, John Seely Brown and Paul Duguid (2000) look at the reasons why information has been elevated to an intellectual pedestal and something that we consume as if in a race against time. They try to change the way we look at information by arguing that information is not, as the 'info-enthusiasts' suggest, a question of bits and bytes stored in databases. Instead, information should be understood within the rich contexts of its circulation among people who use it. That use is creative. Information is transformed by human beings, through interactions in social contexts, into usable knowledge. It is those social contexts that structure the ways in which we use information and learn.

This is a completely different way of understanding information flows and it allows us to see how unhelpful it is to think that we are doomed to drown in the information deluge. If we pay attention to the 'social life of information' we begin to realise that 'the way forward is, paradoxically, to look not ahead but to look around' (Brown and Duguid 2000: 3). If we do that, we can start to understand and use our information technologies in a more holistic and, arguably, humane way. The social life of information reminds us that information is embedded in social contexts. If we begin to apply that idea to our understanding of the Web as a network of platforms for the circulation of simultaneous conversations, then we begin to see that perhaps the metaphor of 'overload' is misplaced.

We go to a party. It's a big room. We could be overwhelmed if we thought that all these people needed to be 'accessed'. Instead, we involve ourselves in conversation, first with one group then perhaps with another. Our involvement screens out the existence of the other, perhaps, two hundred people in the room. In theory, we *could* speak to everyone – running around like some crazed socialite ticking off a list. But that is not how we would react. Our challenge when faced with this context is to decide which conversations to join. We normally start with the people we know.

This is largely what we do as we use the Internet. The confusing aspect is in thinking that the public conversations that are taking place on these platforms are actually aimed at you. *Facebook* or *Twitter* conversations can seem trivial if you are not part of them. But they are significant if you are. Thinking of the Web as conversation and information as social means that, instead of worrying about overload, turning off and hunkering down, we will look for our own place in those conversations. We extend them and transform the social information into applicable knowledge.

We have often been asked by some more sceptical colleagues why we blog and use a variety of social media platforms in our work as teachers, lecturers and writers. Why bother putting up a blog post or web page when there are so many others that deal with the topic in such a better way? Our answer is that, by contributing, we are joining the conversation and, by joining the conversation, each time we do so, we are changing the way that we think about information. We are not riding a tsunami; instead, we are enjoying some fascinating conversations through which we transform information into knowledge.

Connecting with others

Humans seem to share an inherent sociability – a tendency to connect and cooperate. Some studies suggest that the tendency to organise with people beyond our immediate family group is hard-wired into our DNA and is the reason for *Homo sapiens*' evolutionary advantage over Neanderthals more than 30,000 years ago (Dunbar 1996). Cliques, clubs, communities, households, gangs and mobs are just some of the groups to which we belong and through which we develop ties through social relations. Those social relations make of every group a social network. For hundreds of years these social networks were formed and developed exclusively through face-to-face encounters. Because of this, the networks remained place-based. In particular, network ties were formed among friends, neighbours and work colleagues – between those within a geographically bounded community where the exchange of information and the sharing of gossip could *only* take place face to face. Such a community is difficult to imagine now. Place-based networks still exist, of course, but they are interlaced with other networks, the ties of which are maintained through communication technologies. Cars, trains, boats and planes allow us to connect to others in ways that loosen the place-based networks. The telegraph, telephone, radio and television have had, and continue to have, a similar effect.

Life is, in this sense, a social network. Tim Berners-Lee recognised this and, by designing the Web, gave us the tools for organising that network. The Web simply makes it easier to make more connections. We now have so many potential connections to so many people to do so many things that it can be, at best, confusing. Of course, there is still a limit to the number of genuine connections one person can have with others, but as communities connect to communities that limit is disappearing. We have seen this with the rise of *Facebook*, currently the number one aggregator of community hubs.

There is an ongoing debate about the significance of this ubiquitous connecting. Some argue that the Internet is harming community life and social relationships and that we are becoming more socially isolated (though networked) individuals as we open up the laptop/mobile phone, plug into our iPods and stare into the middle distance (Kraut et al. 1998; Turkle 2011). Others suggest that the family, that group which perhaps more than any other constitutes our most significant social connections, is actually benefiting from these new digitally networked channels of communication. A 2008 report from the Pew Internet & American Life Project found that 'Technology is enabling new forms of family connectedness that revolve around remote cell phone interactions and communal internet experiences' (Kennedy and Pew Internet & American Life Project, 2008: ii).

Although there is debate about the *quality* of the connections and their effects, there is no doubt that we are connecting more and more often from more places and over greater distances than ever before. Whether with family and friends, or communities of interest, passion or purpose, we are using the tools and the infrastructure available to us in order to communicate and, by doing so, to form groups and do things.

We have connected to old friends through *Facebook* and made new connections for teaching projects. We have brought colleagues into the classroom with *Skype* when they have been away at conferences. We have invited colleagues who live and work in other countries to share their research and ideas with us here at the university, and invited school groups to participate in seminars with our students, asking questions and getting a feel for university life. And we have only scratched the surface in both the uses and meanings of such communication possibilities. Indeed, the always-on, mobile communication society is a dynamic site for study, learning and understanding, which is moving at breakneck speed and suggesting some fundamental changes for the future:

> The mobile's remarkable processing power (both on the handset and over the network) is bringing data, images, music, and videos to our fingertips; as we become closer to our 'data', our memories, our work and our surveillance of our social environment are mediated by our handsets, and our mobiles alter our experience of mind.
>
> (Ling and Donner 2009: 106)

Summary

In this chapter we have reviewed the impacts of new forms of communication and media on society. New publishing paradigms, changes in the ways we get things done, an acceleration of information flows and an increase in the connections between people are all having profound effects on people and institutions. So far, we have only touched on some of the consequences that these changes are having on education. In the next chapter we will delve more deeply into those consequences and begin to chart the emergence of new stories about education, teaching and learning.

Discussion points

- As you were reading through the case studies and ideas within this chapter, which of them rang true with your own life experiences with technology outside formal education?

- To what extent does formal education within the school seek to adopt some of the processes that technology has facilitated in wider society? What are the potential barriers that restrict these processes?

Useful websites/resources

http://ccmixter.org   *ccMixter* home page
http://craphound.com   Cory Doctorow's craphound.com
http://en.wikipedia.org/wiki/Wikipedia:Neutral_point_of_view
'Wikipedia: neutral point of view' article

Notes

1 www.xtranormal.com.
2 www.youtube.com/watch?hl=en-GB&v=obTNwPJv018.
3 www.xtranormal.com.
4 http://ccmixter.com.
5 www.musicianlink.com.
6 http://upload.wikimedia.org/wikipedia/foundation/5/5c/WP_Key_Facts_feb_2010.pdf, 7 http://en.wikipedia.org/wiki/Wikipedia:Size_comparisons.
7 www.alexa.com/topsites.
8 http://en.wikipedia.org/w/index.php?title=Wikipedia:Wikipedia_as_a_press_source&oldid=419153948.
9 http://en.wikipedia.org/w/index.php?title=Wikipedia:Wikipedia_as_an_academic_source&oldid=421190649.
10 http://en.wikipedia.org/w/index.php?title=Wikipedia:Wikipedia_as_a_court_source&oldid=402512985.
11 www.telegraph.co.uk/education/6943325/Schoolchildren-told-to-avoid-Wikipedia.html.
12 www.guardian.co.uk/education/2007/feb/07/highereducation.historyand historyofart.
13 http://wikileaks.ch.
14 http://en.wikipedia.org/w/index.php?title=Wikipedia:Neutral_point_of_view&oldid=427388650.

References

Brown, J. S. and Duguid, P. (2000) *The Social Life of Information*, Boston, MA: Harvard Business School Press.

Bruns, A. (2008) *Blogs, Wikipedia, Second Life, and Beyond: From production to produsage*, New York: Peter Lang.

Carr, N. (2008) *The Big Switch: Rewiring the world from Edison to Google*, New York: W. W. Norton.

Doctorow, C. (2003) *Down and Out in the Magic Kingdom*, New York: Tor Books.

Doctorow, C. (2009) 'Locus online features: Cory Doctorow: writing in the age of distraction', *Locus*. Available online: www.locusmag.com/Features/2009/01/cory-doctorow-writing-in-age-of.html (accessed 9 May 2011).

Dunbar, R. I. M. (1996) *Grooming, Gossip, and the Evolution of Language*, Cambridge, MA: Harvard University Press.

Frick, T. (1984) 'J. G. Ballard, The Art of Fiction No. 85', *The Paris Review*. Available online: www.theparisreview.org/interviews/2929/the-art-of-fiction-no-85-j-g-ballard (accessed 9 May 2011).

Friedman, T. (2007) *The World is Flat: The globalized world in the twenty-first century*, London: Penguin.

Gee, J. (2004) *Situated Language and Learning: A critique of traditional schooling*, London: Routledge.

Giles, J. (2005) 'Internet encyclopaedias go head to head', *Nature*, 438: 900–1.

Hilbert, M. and Lopez, P. (2011) 'The world's technological capacity to store, communicate, and compute information', *Science*, 332: 60–5.

Kennedy, T. L. M. and Pew Internet & American Life Project (2007) 'Networked families parents and spouses are using the internet and cell phones to create a "new connectedness" that builds on remote connections and shared internet experiences'. Washington, DC: Pew Internet & American Life Project. Available online: www.pewinternet.org/~/media/Files/Reports/2008/PIP_Networked_Family.pdf.pdf (accessed 5 December 2011).

Kraut, R., Patterson, M., Lundmark, V., Kiesler, S., Mukopadhyay, T. and Scherlis, W. (1998) 'Internet paradox: a social technology that reduces social involvement and psychological well-being?', *The American Psychologist*, 53: 1017–31.

Lanier, J. (2010) *You Are Not a Gadget: A manifesto*, London: Penguin.

Leadbeater, C. and Miller, P. (2004) *The Pro-Am Revolution*, London: Demos. Available online: www.demos.co.uk/files/proamrevolutionfinal.pdf?1240939425 (accessed 5 December 2011).

Ling, R. S. and Donner, J. (2009) *Mobile Communication*, Cambridge: Polity.

Lyman, P., Varian, H. R., Swearingen, K., Charles, P., Good, N., Jordan, L. L. and Pal, J. (2003) *How Much Information? 2003*, Berkeley, CA: School of Information Management and Systems, University of California at Berkeley. Available online: www.sims.berkeley.edu/research/projects/how-much-info-2003 (accessed 5 December 2011).

Ofcom (2010) *The Communications Market 2010: Internet and web-based content*. Available online: http://stakeholders.ofcom.org.uk/binaries/research/cmr/753567/UK-internet.pdf (accessed 9 May 2011).

Sellers, S. (2006) 'Rattling other people's cages: the J.G. Ballard interview', *Ballardian*. Available online: www.ballardian.com/rattling-other-peoples-cages-the-jg-ballard-interview (accessed 9 May 2011).

Shirky, C. (2008) *Here Comes Everybody*, New York: Allen Lane.

Sifrey, M. L. (2011) *Wikileaks and the Age of Transparency*, New Haven, CT: Yale University Press.

Turkle, S. (2011) *Alone Together: Why we expect more from technology and less from each other*, New York: Basic Books.

3

Towards participation

Key questions

- To what extent are terms like digital native or digital immigrant helpful in defining ourselves as users of technology?

- How do the terms of digital inclusion, digital life skills and digital media literacy relate to the practice of education in today's schools?

- What types of digital skills do young people exhibit in their wider lives? How can we begin to build on these within educational settings?

- How can we build in various digital literacies within our work as teachers?

As we have discussed in the previous chapter, digital technologies permeate our lives in the twenty-first century. Schools have had to respond to these technological changes. The political and cultural pressures on them are considerable. This chapter examines a number of assumptions surrounding the use of digital technologies in our broader culture. It considers the claim that young people are naturally net savvy, while older generations are always somehow left behind and unable to catch up; it explores what young people do online and the social skills and understandings they are developing; and it considers what 'literacy' looks like in a digital age and how we might think about it in our own lives and work. Finally, we look at how we as educators can support young people in becoming full participants in public and community life.

Digital participation: the context

Knowing how to use digital technologies is commonly accepted as being essential to living and working in a networked society. It is often expressed as a need to respond to the very new demands of a 'knowledge economy' (Barney 2001: 77–83) or 'information society' (Castells 2003: 65–70). In the United Kingdom, the imperative to develop a knowledge economy was clear in the 1998 White Paper, *Our Competitive Future: Building the knowledge driven economy* (DTI 1998). Two elements emerge in that paper that have become recurring themes throughout the last 20 years. The first is the idea that fostering innovation is central to economic success and the second is that education should be closely linked to the needs of new enterprises: education must feed the knowledge economy and at the same time incorporate the tools of that economy, principally technology, in order to facilitate the kinds of lifelong and distance learning that it was argued were central to a dynamic, constantly changing world. What to feed and how to feed that knowledge economy has become the central concern of government education policy since the late 1990s. Very quickly it was seen that, if the economy was to be a network economy, there would be an overriding need to provide a more solid and expanded network infrastructure, enable increased access and maximise the effect of that access to technology for all citizens.

Reflective task

What have been the consequences of government policies aimed at meeting the demands of a 'knowledge economy' within the educational context where you work? Consider:

- the ways in which your role as a teacher has been defined, developed or changed in recent years;

- the resources that you work with, the infrastructure that is available for you and your pupils, or other physical, environmental consequences;

- the curriculum frameworks that you work with, or have seen emerge and develop in recent years;

- the changing sets of skills that your pupils bring with them to the classroom environment, i.e. how have they, your pupils, responded to these new opportunities and access?

Digital Britain

In 2008, Lord Carter, Minister for Communications, Technology and Broadcasting, began a consultation process that, it was hoped, would provide a blueprint for enabling the UK to capitalise on digital technologies. *Digital Britain: Final report* (DCMS/BIS 2009) covered such things as commitments to increasing broadband speed, improving Internet regulation, particularly over piracy and intellectual property theft, and public service broadcasting. The report was widely criticised, especially by those who felt that the speed and reach of broadband had not been addressed and that the heavy hand of state regulation on issues such as copyright were imposing standards inimical to innovation. What the report did, however, and what was later included in the 2010 Digital Economy Act, was to establish a 'National Plan for Digital Participation', which would increase 'the reach, breadth and depth of digital technology use across all sections of society, to maximise digital participation and the economic and social benefits it can bring' (ibid.: 41). In other words, here was a plan to make the UK 'net savvy'. It would be fostered through 'digital inclusion', developed with 'digital life skills' and crowned by 'digital media literacy'.

This insistence on digital inclusion, digital life skills and digital media literacy has had important repercussions in education. In response to inclusion (the idea of universal access to digital technologies, including broadband), there continues to be an expansion of digital technologies in schools. Digital life skills (skills that increase social and employment opportunities) have led to ICT becoming embedded in the National Curriculum, introduced at a younger and younger age, and extended through provision to the elderly in a variety of settings.

Digital media literacy, the most contested and in some ways the least tangible of these imperatives, is seen as crucially important. The *Digital Britain* report looked to Ofcom to recommend a new definition and ambition for a 'National Media Literacy Plan' through the work of a new group, the Digital Media Literacy Working Group.

In its articulation of digital media literacy, the report of the working group focuses on media literacy, recognising it as a useful technical term:

> There is no single, agreed definition of media literacy. Media literacy is an umbrella term covering a set of personal skills, knowledge and understanding of media and communications. It is a specialist term, not part of everyday language.

(Ofcom 2009: 4)

It goes on to acknowledge that there are two other non-traditional literacies that appear in public and educational policy: digital literacy and information literacy:

> Information literacy and digital literacy include within their definitions some of the competencies related to skills, knowledge and understanding included

in media literacy. Some authors suggest that media literacy is simply literacy in the context of the digital world. Others relate it to 21st century literacy.

(ibid.)

It concludes by describing digital media literacy as a subset of media literacy. Media literacy is defined as 'the ability to use, understand and create media and communications', while digital media literacy is 'the ability to use, understand and create digital media and communications'. In that report, advice is offered on the best ways to achieve what is described as a step change in the delivery of media literacy to ensure 'a population that is confident and empowered to access, use and create digital media' (ibid.: 34).

This, then, is the political context within which digital networked technologies must be understood, including their importance in education and schools. 'Literacy' emerges as a central imperative from this context. However, before we examine media literacy and digital media literacy there are two issues that need to be explored. The first concerns the extent to which young people can be understood as already-literate digital 'natives', while the second questions what is meant by participation in online worlds by young people.

Practical task

- Next time you have the opportunity, ask your pupils what they think being digitally 'literate' means? Is this a term they understand naturally? Are they able to define it easily? Or do you just get a lot of bemused faces?

- Spend a few moments considering your own definition for 'digital literacy'. How does it compare or contrast with those provided by your pupils?

Digital natives

How do you respond to the following claims?

- Digital technologies are part of young people's lifestyle and everyday experience.

- The part that such technologies play in their lives is different from the part it plays in your life.

- You are a little in awe of, perhaps intimidated by, their abilities with new digital technologies.

- Young people are reliant on digital technologies in ways that you are not.
- Young people are natural and inveterate multitaskers.
- They are constantly connected and constantly communicating.
- The majority of young people expect their worlds, in schools and out, to be saturated with digital technology.

If you found yourself agreeing with the majority of them, then you may also agree with the ideas of a number of commentators who have argued that young people growing up with digital technology, who network and collaborate and respond to the demands of a digital age, constitute a distinct generation variously described as 'Generation Y', the 'Millennials' or the 'Net Generation'. This generation, it is argued, born between 1980 and 1994 and exposed to digital technologies since birth, think and process information in fundamentally different ways than older generations. It is a generation, according to the title of one book, that is *Growing Up Digital* (Tapscott 1998); of another, that has been *Born Digital* (Palfrey and Gasser 2008); and of a third, that has spawned a new species, *Homo zappiens* (Veen and Vrakking 2006).

One argument in particular, which emerged at the beginning of the century, has been influential. Marc Prensky has suggested that the technological fluency of this generation means that 'they are all "native speakers" of the digital language of computers, video games and the internet' (Prensky 2001: 1), while older generations are 'digital immigrants'.

These metaphors, the digital native/digital immigrant, fuel debates not only about the relations between young people and their technologies, adults and children, but, perhaps more importantly, about radically changing education and in particular rethinking the role of the teacher.

The 'native' belongs, occupies her or his proper place, by virtue of a random condition (such as place or date of birth) whereas the immigrant is the outsider, the person who comes from another country with the intention of settling. Two curious elements of the metaphor give us pause: the settler cannot truly settle without the acceptance of the native; the settler, by definition, can never meet the conditions to become a native. You can learn a second language but never become a native speaker of that language.

When Prensky suggests that 'our students have changed radically. Today's students are no longer people our educational system was designed to teach' (ibid.), we, as immigrants, are implicitly urged to change our practices in order to accommodate the new learning styles of a generation from whom we are divided. When Veen and Vrakking, who describe the digital natives as '*Homo zappiens*', suggest that this new generation considers schools as 'disconnected institutions, more or less irrelevant to them as far as their daily life is concerned' and that they 'want to be in control of what they engage with and do not possess the patience to listen to a teacher explaining the world as it is according to him/her' (2006: 10), we are challenged to act.

The conundrum for education, according to this view, is how we might bridge that generational divide. How can digital settlers integrate with digital natives in ways that they can both speak the same language, albeit perhaps with different accents? Can the digital immigrant teacher accommodate to the digital native learner and how can schools become more relevant to the lives of the young people they teach? Or should these immigrants simply 'get out of the way' and let the learners learn?

This view of digital natives has gained currency in the past ten years and it is tempting to accept it as a given. We all know some young people who correspond in many ways to the kinds of young people described as digital natives. Indeed Tom, whom we met in Chapter 2, would certainly seem to be a candidate for inclusion, although I think he might draw the line at being described as a *Homo zappiens*! As intuitively attractive as it may be, however, is it actually accurate? Is the 'digital native' sobriquet simply part of a commercial strategy that flatters a whole generation in order that they buy into its technological novelties? Could it be that the digital immigrant is thereby offered a legitimate excuse for not engaging with such novelty?

In one review of this evidence it was found that both the skills in, and experience of, digital technologies among young people are far from universal (Bennett et al. 2008). How teenagers use technology is influenced by age group, socio-economic background, cultural/ethnic background and gender. It appears that the digital native group is more heterogeneous than it is perceived to be by the advocates of digital nativeness: 'It may be that there is as much variation *within* the digital native generation as between the generations' (ibid.: 779). Nor can learning styles be understood as uniform, static or generalisable across this generation. To suggest that a particular group favours a particular learning style is to gloss over the ways in which people of all ages modify their learning strategies according to particular tasks in particular places and for particular purposes. It also fails to take into account research that reports children's more passive interactions with the Web (Livingstone 2009). Being able to use a Web-browser does not make you a digital native: at least one as described by Prensky (2001), Veen and Vrakking (2006) and Tapscott (1998).

Uncovering the problematic assumptions about digital natives has been paralleled by research into its complement, the digital immigrant. Many such immigrants have been using digital technologies for over 30 years. They use them differently, which is unsurprising. They most probably use their cars differently, have different interests from teenagers and think about things in different ways than teenagers do. This is reflected in their use of digital technologies, particularly online, where older adults spend less time on entertainment and social networking and more time on conducting research, shopping and banking (Jones et al. 2009). Trends reported by Ofcom suggest that the generational divide is actually narrowing significantly and rapidly (Ofcom 2010).

If the distinction between natives and immigrants is more myth than reality, more simplistic than nuanced, what then is the reality of young people's use and understandings of digital networked technologies?

Hanging out, messing around and geeking out: young people's use of technology

In the UK, research conducted at Futurelab,[1] Becta[2] (British Educational Communications and Technology Agency) and the Oxford Institute of Internet Studies[3] suggests that young people's use of digital technologies informally (in the home, in leisure sites, etc.) is, in some significant sense, creating very different worlds than those created by the use of technology in formal education. A Becta-funded project, *The Learner and their Context*, tentatively links the power of technology to engage and empower young people at home to benefits in learning:

> In respect to both formal and informal learning broadly, it appears that there is some evidence from our findings to suggest that sustained access to new technologies in the home is associated in a number of cases with increasingly engaging and empowering experiences of learning.
>
> (Davies et al. 2008: 45)

But what exactly is this engagement? How are young people empowered? What are the different worlds that are being created? What do young people *do* with digital networked technologies and what does what they do *mean* for them?

In *Hanging Out, Messing Around, and Geeking Out* (Ito 2009), researchers from the John D. and Catherine T. MacArthur Foundation offer some fascinating insights into these questions in a framework that enables us to throw light on our second concern in this chapter – the nature of digital participation and what it means for young people.

Hanging Out, Messing Around, and Geeking Out is a report of a three-year, large-scale ethnographic study into young people's learning in informal settings. It involved 28 researchers, 7,000 interviews and over 5,000 hours of observation off- and online. Rather than beginning with preset categories, the researchers used interviewing, observation and interpretive analysis to understand cultural patterns and social practices from the point of view of young people themselves. In such ethnographic research, grounded in fieldwork, context is vital. Patterns and practices emerge from a context in which peer relations, family dynamics, communities, institutions and wider cultural networks all play a role.

Hanging out ...

From this research, Ito and her team describe three 'genres of participation' through which young people engage with media. The first, 'hanging out', involves maintaining social connections with friends. For teenagers, online and offline worlds are seamlessly integrated in media-saturated, always-on, 'hyper-social' worlds.

Through participation in social network sites such as *MySpace*, *Facebook* and *Bebo* (among others), as well as instant and text messaging, young people are constructing new social norms and forms of media literacy in networked public culture that reflect the enhanced role of media in their lives. (Ito 2009: 13)

Rarely, however, is such hanging out seen by parents or schools as supporting learning. That seamless integration of online and offline connection is often not recognised as social or learning at all. Offline hanging out is restricted (classrooms and parents get in the way) and the online is likely to be heavily policed. This is because *Facebook*, *YouTube*, *IM* and text messaging are readily characterised as cause for concern for parents and teachers. This anecdote from Susan Maushart describing the social habits of her three teenagers is typical of this kind of response:

> They were still having friends over, but more and more of their socialis-ing took the form of little knots of spectators gathered around the cheery glow of *YouTube* – or worse, dispersed into separate corners, each to his own device. Their sleep patterns were heading south too – hardly surprising given that the alerts from their three cell phones were intermittently audible throughout the night, chirping like a cadre of evil crickets.
>
> (Maushart 2011: 13)

Such popular accounts, and there are many, fail to do justice to the significance of hanging out, which, according to Ito, is the first stage of learning how to be with others in digital spaces. Young people learn the skills of maintaining social network profiles, as well as uploading and downloading content, as social prac-tices, not technological tasks. As with children in early childhood centres, the emphasis is on understanding how you relate to others.

Messing around ...

The second genre of participation, 'messing around', raises the stakes:

> Unlike hanging out, in which the desire is to maintain social connections to friends, messing around represents the beginning of a more intense, media-centric form of engagement. When messing around, young people begin to

take an interest in and focus on the workings and content of technology and media themselves, tinkering, exploring and extending their understanding.

(Ito 2009: 20)

Messing around is centred on play and experimentation and is largely self-directed and self-taught. Searching for content, creating, editing and sharing photos and videos are examples of messing around. They are learning contexts that emerge from personal interest and, although not necessarily goal-directed, can open up new forms and levels of engagement. Such contexts are more often supported by peers who share the same interests and can help novices to improve their technical skills. It is the kind of learning that can enable young teenagers to be given the role of technical expert in the home or even in the classroom. Messing about is still social, but the personal interests that led to play and experimentation become drivers of personal development that, while shared socially, go beyond the immediately social. The emphasis moves from how you relate to others through friendship towards how friendship networks can help to develop your own interests.

Geeking out …

The third and final genre of participation, 'geeking out', is described as:

an intense commitment to or engagement with media or technology, often one particular media property, genre or type of technology. Geeking out involves learning to navigate esoteric domains of knowledge and practice and participating in communities that traffic in these forms of expertise. It is a mode of learning that is peer-driven, but focused on gaining deep knowledge and expertise in specific areas of interest.

(Ito 2009: 28)

Geeking out happens when an interest becomes a passion and self-directed learning takes place in collaborative spaces of shared passions. Geeking out is not, according to Ito's research, a solitary activity. Instead, it is deeply embedded in networks of sharing, cooperation and collaboration that reach beyond local friendship networks or peer groups. It is in geeking out that new knowledge is created in online networks that 'provide an opportunity for youth to exercise adult-like agency and leadership that is not otherwise available to them' (ibid.: 30). The emphasis in geeking out moves beyond 'interest' to passion and an intrinsic motivation to learn more, share more and participate in knowledge networks where that participation is recognised and validated by the community.

What this approach to young people's media use does is to emphasise the ways in which young people participate with online media and how they understand that participation. It is a method that looks at an overall ecology of media that is constantly changing as people develop new modes of communication and culture through media technologies. Hanging out can lead to messing around. The practices involved in messing around can lead to geeking out. Such genres illustrate various forms of being and learning through digital networked technologies.

While this research shows that young people do know a great deal about the media environments they participate in, it does not recommend that, as educators or parents, we cannot support their learning in such environments and help them to engage critically with their use of media.

To give one small example, many young people are adept at hanging out on *Facebook*. They are fluent in the social norms that shape interaction. Some mess around. They upload, share and re-purpose content on their profile pages. If, however, you ask these same young people what *Facebook* is for, they will most probably reply 'for making friends'. What they are less likely to appreciate is that *Facebook* exists to monetise the connections that are made every time they 'friend' or are 'friended'. Those connections and the information that you tell those friends are deposited with *Facebook*: Mark Zuckerberg (the Chief Executive and President of *Facebook*) is everyone's friend on the site and he is not the easiest of friends to leave. He guards your information, photographs, likes and dislikes, intimate details and friendship network, because it is potentially powerful information. This is the kind of critical perspective that young people sometimes struggle with and where teachers and parents can assist. We will return to the importance of this kind of critical engagement in Chapter 6.

Practical task

What are the consequences of hanging out, messing around and geeking out for how you might design a specific teaching activity within a lesson? Can you identify general themes, tentative approaches or specific actions that you can take from the above discussion and apply to your work? If so, why not take one of them and use it to help inform the planning for a specific teaching activity to include within a lesson?

Media literacies

Ito (2009) and her research team describe the social norms and practices that young people engage in and offer a framework for thinking about how they progress through genres of participation. In a parallel report, *Confronting the Challenges of Participatory Culture*, Henry Jenkins (2009) draws out the new media literacies that these social practices embody. He describes them as follows:

- *Play* – the capacity to experiment with your surroundings as a form of problem-solving.

- *Performance* – the ability to adopt alternative identities for the purpose of improvisation and discovery.

- *Simulation* – the ability to interpret and construct dynamic models of real-world processes.

- *Appropriation* – the ability meaningfully to sample and remix media content.

- *Multitasking* – the ability to scan one's environment and shift focus as needed to salient details.

- *Distributed cognition* – the ability to interact meaningfully with tools that expand mental capacities.

- *Collective intelligence* – the ability to pool knowledge and compare notes with others towards a common goal.

- *Judgement* – the ability to evaluate the reliability and credibility of different information sources.

- *Transmedia navigation* – the ability to follow the flow of stories and information across multiple modalities.

- *Networking* – the ability to search for, synthesise and disseminate information across multiple modalities.

- *Negotiation* – the ability to travel across diverse communities, discerning and respecting multiple perspectives, and grasping and following alternative norms.

Instead of thinking about literacy as a competence that someone has, Jenkins' framework encompasses a number of cultural and social skills that are necessary for full participation in communities. Supporting young people towards such full participation lies at the heart of both education and parenting. Some teachers are incorporating these skills into classrooms both with and in the absence of digital networked technologies – these skills are not dependent on digital networked technologies, nor are they limited to ICT classes.

These new media literacies are not intended to replace 'older' literacies but rather supplement them. So:

- *Traditional literacy* is still important. Competence in reading and writing and an understanding of the social nature of texts continues to be instrumental to educational development.

- *Information literacy*, which emerged from information science and librarianship and which emphasises when information is necessary and when not, as well as how to discover particular information for particular purposes, constitutes a vital research skill.

- *Technical literacy*, often included in ICT and which involves the expertise necessary to use computer hardware and software effectively, is still indispensable.

- *Critical skills* are still vital for engaging with texts and understanding the institutional/political economy in which they are produced and consumed.

- *Visual literacy* allows us to navigate the multiple modalities in which visual representations are created.

Practical task

The challenge for us, as teachers, is to consider how we can build opportunities for these literacies to develop in our pupils. To what extent are you building these different types of literacies into your own teaching practice? Why not review a standard unit of work that you teach? Highlight the opportunities that you have to teach the different literacies, or provide opportunities for pupils to demonstrate them in their work. Are there any that are missing? Why not choose one and try to emphasise it more strongly in a lesson or two that you teach over the coming week?

Learning literacies

Jenkins (2009) focuses his report on participatory cultures, digital participation and those literacies that are essential for young people to become full participants. However, such literacies are not exclusive to young people. As we noted in our discussion of the *Digital Britain* report, the imperative to participate is aimed at the whole population. In thinking about new literacies for young people we would do well to think about our own literacy practices and the cultures of participation in which we are, or might be, involved.

We have to be learners before we are teachers. This does not mean we are advocating yet more 'professional development courses' and support (although such courses and support may play a part). Instead, as we discussed in the introduction to this chapter, we need to develop the deeper cultural skills, knowledge and understandings that can only be acquired by 'being there'. We need to become fieldworkers in our own literacy practices as we play with, experiment with, share and collaborate in the social practices of the new cultures that are emerging online. In this way we can begin to move away from the sometimes prevailing view that digital networked technologies are simply tools. In one sense they are tools. But, much more importantly, digital networked technologies are processes – ways of being, of thinking, of organising and of doing – that can only be understood from the inside.

In order to complete our description of participatory media and media literacy let us now share our literacy fieldwork notes of 'being there' in one particular culture of participation: the Twittersphere.

Twitter

As we write this, *Twitter* is five years old. Simply put, *Twitter* is a social network that revolves around short messages (tweets) of 140 characters. That network is made up of you plus the people you follow and those who follow you. Your main *Twitter* page is a list of tweets from the people you follow appearing in reverse chronological order. Those tweets consist of updates on thoughts, ideas and activities posted through a browser or mobile device. When it launched, the site's prompt question for its users was, 'What are you doing?' Most of the time 'what we do' is fairly trivial: 'eating in the canteen' or 'waiting for Jenny' are banal excerpts of a life that, taken singly, have little significance. However, by 2007/8 some people began to see that there was something to this network communication beyond its addictive quality for an always-on generation of early adopters.

When *Twitter* changed its prompt question in 2009 to 'What's happening?', it recognised that its users had created an information network that had quickly grown beyond personal status updates. Because it was an open system, it was the users who drove this change; the owners of *Twitter* responded.

With its 'What's happening?' prompt, *Twitter*'s focus harnessed both the power of personal witness and the power of networks to coordinate collective activity. The network effect was destined to be significant with the staggering growth in the numbers of people using *Twitter* and the level of their engagement with the service. One billion tweets are sent per week; 177 million tweets were sent on 11 March 2011; and 572,000 new accounts were created on 12 March 2011 (*Twitter* 2011). *Twitter* is used for a variety of purposes and within a variety of contexts. It was *Twitter* that provided the BBC with its first news of the earthquake in China in 2008, suggesting that the '*Twitter* fad' had come of age (Cellan-Jones 2008). It is claimed to have had a significant role to play in political activism throughout the world and the phrase '*Twitter* revolution' has been applied to uprisings and campaigns of civil resistance in Moldova, Egypt, Tunisia and Iran (Hands 2011).

No marketing company is complete without a '*Twitter* strategy' and newspaper press rooms are incomplete without a '*Twitter* feed' streaming in updates on various topics and breaking news. With the use of hashtags (#), topics become shared and more visible, as well as allowing direct communication between members of social groups and organisations. Placing # before or after a message enables followers of that hashtag to monitor updates even if they do not follow the person sending the tweet. Because *Twitter* has been built on open-source software, hundreds of tools and applications have been created to integrate *Twitter* with other services and make it easier to use. As the numbers using *Twitter* grow, so too do these tools and applications.

Case study 3.1: My use of *Twitter*

I started using *Twitter* on 5 July 2008 with the tweet shown in Figure 3.1.

waldenpond Clive McGoun
An experiment in micro-diary writing. A tweet a day to chart my thoughts/actions over a period of time. Exploring the pond that is Waldon.
5 Jul 08

Figure 3.1 The author's first tweet

That afternoon, as I was looking at the *Twitter* sign-up page, I had been reading Thoreau's *Walden* (about his life at Walden Pond) and chose the username 'waldenpond'; hence, that final sentence. Significantly, I had understood *Twitter* as a micro-blog, a personal diary, to record 'what I was doing' and build up a picture of a life over time in pithy mini-posts. I hung out. I spent time choosing the people to follow. I 'unfollowed' many. I watched the ways in which others used *Twitter*. I imitated some behaviour and ignored other behaviour. I spent months obsessively tweeting. Other months I tweeted less. Above all, I integrated *Twitter* into my professional and personal life in ways that led to many benefits. Above all, I learned from others.

My attraction to *Twitter* was eloquently summarised in a blog post by Howard Rheingold (2009), a digital visionary who compiled a list of reasons why he used *Twitter*. Here is his list with some glosses:

- *Openness*: anyone can join *Twitter* and (if required by the user, request to) follow anyone else.
- *Immediacy*: this is real-time, synchronous, flowing communication – a conversation with multiple participants.
- *Variety*: the flavour of the conversation can be modified through the people and topics you select in the conversation.
- *Reciprocity*: people give and ask for information freely.
- *A channel to multiple publics*: because of the networks that you create and participate in, the news you want to broadcast can be distributed efficiently and effectively.

- *Asymmetry*: we rarely follow the same people who follow us. This is not a mutual follower–followed network. Viewing our networks can be a little surprising.

- *A way to meet new people*: the Internet has always been about connecting people with shared interests. *Twitter* is another tool to do that.

- *A window on what is happening in multiple worlds*: we can dip our toes in worlds that we may be curious about without plumbing the depths.

- *Community-forming*: *Twitter* has space for the kinds of idle chat that ties groups together.

- *A platform for mass collaboration*: there are hundreds of examples of how *Twitter* has been used in this way.

- *Searchability*: *Twitter* allows for real-time searches on topics.

The benefits Rheingold experiences from using *Twitter* are directly related to the selection of people he follows and how he caters for the people who follow him: 'I think the successful use of *Twitter* means knowing how to tune the network of people you follow and how to feed the network of people who follow you' (ibid.).

I tried to learn from him. Tuning means following and 'unfollowing'. People often ask 'who do you follow on *Twitter*?' and 'how do you decide who to follow?' The answer is always very personal. I have specific professional interests. I follow people who, in my case, are knowledgeable about education and particularly digital technologies in education. There are less specific professional interests. I follow others who are knowledgeable and experienced about technology and social change. I know they are knowledgeable and experienced because I listen to them and I listen to others who listen to them. I double-check what they say if it is contentious. I also have personal interests that may change over time. I listen to people building canoes, tweeting about their learning experiences and progress; to knowledge communities in Manchester commenting on local creative business initiatives; and to civil activists in Cuba. The people I follow constantly provide links to useful information and, in doing so, act as a kind of recommendation engine for current reading. I thank them when they do. I often ask my networks for resources instead of going to *Google*.

To continue to be useful those networks need to be revised and reconfigured. They constitute dynamic participatory cultures that can bring enormous dividends in terms of personal learning. Finding and sharing with people in your own network leads to information and learning through that network. Understanding who produces what, why and from what point of view applies equally to people in my networks. Choosing who to follow influences the information that flows through the network. Dedicated *Twitter* browsers such as *TweetDeck*[4] help to monitor different flows and switch between them. I share pictures with *Twitpic*,[5] visualise my networks with *Twitter Browser*[6] and watch *Twitter* 'memes' cascading down my screen in real time with *TwitterFall*.[7] I use hashtags to tune into *Twitter* discussions such as #education or the Thursday evening #ukedchat.

Feeding the network is as important as being fed by it. Feeding the network is creating content for others. People follow you because they have identified in your tweets something that attracts them to the conversation. It may be personal. It may be because of your pithy commentary. You might make them laugh. The links you include in your tweets may take them to information they find useful. Whatever that attraction is, it needs to be fed. Because of the multiple audiences that your network encompasses, such feeding may not always be easy. With multiple audiences come multiple conversations and all of those conversations will not be of interest or perhaps appropriate to all. Although I use *Twitter* as a predominantly professional network, I cannot do so without sharing our days, humour and things that are personal to us. It is a social/professional/learning network. Yet it is in the public domain and we are conscious that we have a responsibility both to the people we follow and to those who follow us. I think critically about how we use it and measure that use ethically.

In hanging out and messing around on *Twitter* I have played, performed, multitasked, learned to think with other people as a form of distributed cognition, pooled knowledge with others to solve problems collectively, evaluated sources and learned how to cultivate our networks. Above all, I have had fun and felt we were being creative in conversation and in the production of content.

How then did I transfer the skills and understanding gained through such fieldwork experience into the classroom?

Using *Twitter* in the classroom

Twitter has been largely used within teaching and learning in higher education across the world. It is only just beginning to make an impact on the work of teachers in schools. However, while many of the features of *Twitter* might be duplicated by other social networking software with which young people are more familiar (e.g. *Facebook*), we believe that *Twitter* and other similar technologies can bring new, collaborative dimensions to teaching and learning in your classroom. The following case study explores one example from the MFL classroom.

Case study 3.2: Developing approaches to assessment with *Twitter* in the MFL classroom

One teacher (Blake-Plock 2009) explored how *Twitter* could be used to help build a more collaborative approach to assessment in the class-room. The first activity involved pupils finding all the target language verbs in a selected passage of text. These verbs, along with their definition and function, were then tweeted on a specific *Twitter* feed (displayed on the interactive whiteboard (IWB) in the classroom). Pupils were asked to help each other by making suggestions or correcting each other's work via the *Twitter* feed. More advanced pupils were given the job of explicitly moderating the feed and giving formative feedback to their peers.

The second activity involved using *Twitter* as a tool to collect resources and evaluate them. Pupils were given a specific topic to research on the Internet. Half the class were designated as online researchers. Everything they found, both good and bad, was fed into a *Twitter* feed. The remaining pupils were resource evaluators. They had to evaluate the found resources and feed back their reports, in less than 140 characters, via the same feed. At the end of the lesson, the *Twitter* feed was saved as an interactive document, full of hyperlinks and annotations, which was used in following lessons as a starting point for further research and as an informant to further class discussions.

Finally, *Twitter* was used by this teacher as an aid for pupils when doing translation. Having identified a particular problem (i.e. pupils getting stuck and frustrated when they could not translate a specific word or phrase correctly), this teacher allowed pupils to post questions on a *Twitter* feed. This feed was monitored by the teacher. It allowed the teacher to give pupils feedback directly, but also meant that pupils could help each other too.

This case study shows how *Twitter* can be embedded into the daily processes of teaching and learning in one classroom. There are many other examples that we could have drawn on. Note that some of the processes that *Twitter* enables are similar to those that could be facilitated in other ways. Some are unique to *Twitter* and its functionality. In our experience, pupils find it helpful to have a specific *Twitter* feed for a specific piece of work. This focuses their attention and energy in a positive way. We also note that *Twitter* is probably not the first choice of social media for most young people at the moment. This alternative to more common social media networks (e.g. *Facebook*) may also have its advantages for your work within school.

In our teaching, we use a *Twitter* hashtag for all the courses we teach and tweet updates and resources that we think students would find useful. We also re-tweet any tweets that we think are relevant from our networks to the students. Occasionally we lecture to large groups. When we do so, we set up a 'backchannel' and ask students to tweet questions and comments as the lecture progresses. Everyone can see that backchannel and the questions and comments as they are posted. At the end of a particular section in the lecture we pause and discuss the posts to the backchannel and use them as a way to monitor understanding, identify issues that need further comment, or recognise issues that we can address in another forum. All the tweets in the backchannel are archived for future reference. We have used tweets as a way of brainstorming a particular topic prior to a seminar and use the archive as a prompt at the beginning of the face-to-face session. We encourage students to hang out and mess around with *Twitter* in ways that can improve their own *Twitter* literacy and nurture their own networks.

Above all, we reflect on the tool with our students, sharing with them our fieldwork, looking at what *Twitter* is natively good at and discussing when it might be problematic. When you unleash a network you can never be completely in control of that network. While we never say anything in our online networks that we would not say face to face, our networks are large. Our students often follow who we follow and there may be conversations on those networks that they may find unsettling or misinterpret.

So, *Twitter* has many functions. We have explored some of these above. In addition, you may find *Twitter* helpful to:

- get pupils to know each other better;
- collaborate on specific projects;

- make announcements to your classes at particular moments of the lesson;
- facilitate brainstorming;
- take polls on specific issues or questions (something that many broadcasters do regularly);
- encourage pupils to be brief and concise in their writing;
- follow key professionals and learn more about their working lives;
- follow new stories as they emerge and contrast these with traditional broadcasting channels;
- and much more besides!

Practical task

Why not create your own *Twitter* account today and start the process of engaging with other *Twitter* users? For further advice on specific use of *Twitter* for education, and some more tools to help support your work in this area, see www.onlinecolleges. net/2009/06/08/50-ways-to-use-twitter-in-the-college-classroom/.

Summary

In this chapter we have traced the contexts in which new cultures of learning and participation are emerging. We have seen some of the top-down factors in this shift – those political, social and economic imperatives that are driving change. We have also examined how the social energies of young people, harnessed through their access to digital networked technologies, are creating pressures towards participation and transparency.

We should also be wary of extrapolating too quickly on changes we have described, the effects of which have only begun to be felt in the last 15 years. We are living through a media revolution that is as important as that produced by the printing press. However, we have yet to see the radical changes to education that many believe this revolution will introduce. Is it 'early days' or are schools natively resistant to change? Or is it because schools are doing something beyond knowledge and information production and dissemination that makes them immune to the tide of digitisation?

We can begin to think through some of the questions that the current shifts we have explored in this chapter should pose for schools and teachers. These are the questions that can help us to think about our roles, the roles of new learners and the roles of schools in learning.

We have emphasised that the new media technologies described by Jenkins (2009) do not supplant traditional literacy, research skills, technical savvy or critical thinking. Instead, such literacies supplement many of the skills and understandings that are presently included in, and taught across, school curricula. Similarly, we do not think that the participatory cultures that are emerging will replace schools. They will, though, increasingly supplement the activities and the organisation of activities within schools. Only in this way can we imagine schools being able to prepare young people for the futures that await them.

Discussion points

- How can schools support the development of friendship-based collaborative cultures into interest-based participation and even geeking out?

- How can I begin to use some of these networked tools (e.g. *Twitter* or similar) to bring a more collaborative approach to the teaching and learning that goes on in my classroom?

Useful websites/resources

http://mitpress.mit.edu/catalog/item/default.asp?ttype=2&tid=11889   MIT Press information on Ito's *Hanging Out, Messing Around, and Geeking Out* (2009).
http://newmedialiteracies.org   New Media Literacies home page.
www.twitter.com   *Twitter* home page.

Notes

1   www.futurelab.org.uk/research.
2   Becta closed on 31 March 2011. However, an archive of its research can be found at: http://webarchive.nationalarchives.gov.uk/20110130111510/http://www.becta.org.uk.
3   www.oii.ox.ac.uk/research.
4   www.tweetdeck.com.
5   http://twitpic.com.
6   www.neuroproductions.be/twitter_friends_network_browser.
7   www.twitterfall.com.

References

Barney, D. D. (2004) *The Network Society*, Cambridge: Polity.

Bennett, S., Maton, K. and Kervin, L. (2008) 'The "digital natives" debate: a critical review of the evidence', *British Journal of Educational Technology*, 39: 775–86.

Blake-Plock, S. (2009) 'Best practices in a *Twitter*-enhanced high school classroom', *Teach Paperless*. Available online: http://teachpaperless.blogspot.com/2009/05/best-practices-in-twitter-enhanced-high.html (accessed 5 September 2011).

Castells, M. (2003) *The Internet Galaxy: Reflections on the Internet, business, and society*, Oxford: Oxford University Press.

Cellan-Jones, R. (2008) '*Twitter* and the China earthquake', dot.life – A Blog about Technology from BBC News. Available online: www.bbc.co.uk/blogs/technology/2008/05/twitter_and_the_china_earthqua.html (accessed 9 May 2011).

Davies, C., Carter, A., Cranmer, S., Eynon, R., Furlong, J., Good, J., Hjorth, I. A., Lee, S., Malmberg, L. and Holmes, W. (2008) *The Learner and Their Context: Benefits of ICT use outside formal education*. Interim report for Becta-funded project 'The Learner and Their Context'. Available online: http://dera.ioe.ac.uk/1524/1/becta_2009_learner_context_interim.pdf (accessed 6 December 2011).

DCMS/BIS (Department for Culture, Media and Sport/Department for Business Innovation and Skills) (2009) *Digital Britain: Final report*, London: The Stationery Office. Available online: www.dcms.gov.uk/images/publications/digitalbritain-finalreport-jun09.pdf (accessed 10 May 2011).

DTI (Department of Trade and Industry) (1998) *Our Competitive Future: Building the knowledge driven economy*, London: The Stationery Office.

Hands, J. (2011) @ *is for Activism: Dissent, resistance and rebellion in a digital culture*, London/New York: Pluto.

Ito, M. (2009) *Hanging Out, Messing Around, and Geeking Out: Kids living and learning with new media*, Cambridge, MA: MIT Press.

Jenkins, H. (2009) *Confronting the Challenges of Participatory Culture: Media education for the 21st century*, Cambridge, MA: MIT Press.

Jones, S., Fox, S. and Pew Internet & American Life Project (2009) *Generations Online in 2009*, Washington, DC: Pew Internet & American Life Project. Available online: www.pewinternet.org/~/media//Files/Reports/2009/PIP_Generations_2009.pdf (accessed 6 December 2011).

Livingstone, S. M. (2009) *Children and the Internet: Great expectations, challenging realities*, Cambridge/Malden, MA: Polity.

Maushart, S. (2011) *The Winter of Our Disconnect: How three totally wired teenagers (and a mother who slept with her iPhone) pulled the plug on their technology and lived to tell the tale*, London: Profile.

Ofcom (2009) *Report of the Digital Media Literacy Working Group*, London: Ofcom.

Ofcom (2010) *The Communications Market 2010: Internet and Web-based content*. London: Ofcom. Available online: http://stakeholders.ofcom.org.uk/binaries/research/cmr/753567/UK-internet.pdf (accessed 9 May 2011).

Palfrey, J. G. and Gasser, U. (2008) *Born Digital: Understanding the first generation of digital natives*, New York: Basic Books.

Prensky, M. (2001) 'Digital natives, digital immigrants, part 1', *On the Horizon – The Strategic Planning Resource for Education Professionals*, 9: 1–6.

Rheingold, H. (2009) '*Twitter* literacy (I refuse to make up a twittery name for it)', SFGate Blogs. Available online: www.sfgate.com/cgi-bin/blogs/rheingold/detail?entry_id=39948 (accessed 9 May 2011).

Tapscott, D. (1998) *Growing Up Digital: The rise of the net generation*, New York: McGraw-Hill.

Twitter (2011) *#numbers*. Twitter Blog. Available online: http://blog.twitter.com/2011/03/numbers.html (accessed 9 May 2011).

Veen, W. and Vrakking, B. (2006) *Homo zappiens: Growing up in a digital age*, London: Network Continuum Education.

4

Choosing and using digital technologies

Key questions

- To what extent do the technologies we choose to use in our teaching affect the processes of teaching and learning that they facilitate?

- What do we gain and what do we lose as we adopt specific tools such as the Internet or the word processor within teaching activities?

- How can we understand and build upon the choices that young people make in their use of technology in their wider lives?

- Who should choose what technologies we use in the classroom? What criteria should we judge them by?

Choices are central to everything we do. As teachers, as in our wider lives, the choices we make have consequences. These affect how we teach, how students learn and the interplay between these two interrelated and symbiotic processes. But even talking about teaching and learning in this binary fashion hides a number of important considerations. Not least of these is the context within which teaching and learning take place (Selwyn 2010). The physical space of the classroom and the wider geographical positioning of the school, as well as the sociological mix of students within these spaces, all have their part to play. Teaching and learning are contextualised. Skilful teachers know this. They are able to adjust their pedagogy on a daily basis. Sometimes these changes are radical; often they are minute, perhaps only felt by the individual involved and therefore not easily observable.

As a simple example, consider the weather and its effect on the behaviour of students. There might not be any scientific explanation, but many teachers comment on how students are often more excitable on windy, autumnal days. Folklore or fact? Either way, experienced teachers know how to respond. They make choices about what to do and what to say; teaching and learning continues but perhaps in a slightly different way to how it might have proceeded on a balmy and sunny summer's afternoon.

Perhaps one of the most important sets of choices that teachers have to make relates to the technologies or tools that they use within their classrooms. By tools we mean anything and everything that your classroom contains, even the desks and chairs! Recently, we attended a concert given by the Manchester Camerata, a leading chamber orchestra in the northwest of England. In the first half, the orchestra was seated in the traditional manner; in the second half, for the performance of a Mozart symphony, the chairs were taken away (deliberately) and the orchestra stood to perform the work. What do you think the difference was? For the musicians, there seemed to be a greater sense of freedom and expression. They moved more to the music, often moving together in their various instrumental sections as the conductor guided them through the music. As members of the audience, the music seemed to come alive in a physical and visual sense. One could 'see' as well as 'hear' the shapes of the melody, the patterns of the rhythms and the shapes of the form. We were left wondering whether, if one was blindfolded, you could tell which half of the concert was performed sitting down and which half was performed standing up. Certainly there seemed to be a difference, and all that just from the removal of the chairs.

Similarly, something as basic as tables and chairs has an effect on the processes of teaching and learning that take place in your classroom. Removing them, or perhaps rearranging them, will result in a very different 'feel' and sense of engagement. It will affect the way in which you communicate with your students, in terms of both your body language and your actual speech. It may also affect their sense of the power dynamics within the classroom space. The result may be a more inclusive and accessible space for learning, but it may result in a space in which traditional notions of the 'teacher' and the 'learner' are undermined in an unhelpful manner. Again, the choices that the teacher makes have consequences.

This chapter is about the choices you might make about technology and how these choices result in consequences for the processes of teaching and learning. Our introduction has focused on one, very common, piece of technology: the chair. It is a simple technology. Perhaps you might not have even considered it a 'technology' if it had not been mentioned. But our brief exploration of the chair and its effect on a musical performance shows the consequences that flow from its adoption and use for a particular purpose. What is true for the chair will be the case for any other form of digital technology that you choose to bring and use within your own classroom. Following on from this consideration of the choices teachers make in respect of the technology that is being used within a classroom setting, we will turn our attention to the choices students make. The chapter will end with an examination of the potential conflicts that can emerge between these two sets of choices, and suggest ways in which this conflict can be resolved.

The importance of teacher choice

Teachers have an important, some would say vital, role in choosing the tools through which students learn. Frank Furedi's book *Wasted: Why education isn't educating* (2009) defends the role of adult authority in education. Adults, he says, have an essential role and responsibility in shaping the type of education that young children receive. What Furedi calls an 'ambiguous status enjoyed by the exercise of adult authority' (ibid.: 7) has resulted in a number of negative features in, or influences on, educational practices. These include what Furedi calls 'the downsizing of the academic learning in the school curriculum' (ibid.: 8), a questioning of the term 'teacher' itself and the traditional authority that such a figure ought to carry, a crisis in the socialisation of children and, perhaps the topic of greatest public concern, an undermining of 'authoritative forms of discipline' (ibid.: 9).

While elements of Furedi's thesis undoubtedly have some truth in them, we are left wondering whether he has actually over-egged the pudding a little. Teacher authority does exist in the vast majority of schools, not least in terms of the choice of resources that are provided within the classroom to support teaching and learning. In terms of technology, the majority of today's schools have benefited from a huge investment in ICT during recent years. For some, the availability of technology has ceased to become the issue; what schools and teachers should do with it is increasingly the concern.

Within this context, the choices that teachers make have important consequences. But before we consider these, certain things have already been established within the educational system that we need to recognise.

At a basic level, the technology infrastructure within schools has been established. Today, it is common for secondary schools to have networked computer systems with broadband Internet access, specialist computer suites for the development of ICT skills or accessible for subject teaching when required, smaller numbers of computers located within individual classrooms, IWBs in many teaching spaces, and a whole array of other smaller, portable technologies (including laptop computers, iPods, recording devices, cameras of various types and much more besides).

The extent to which teachers have had a say in the type of ICT provision that their schools have made, the location of these computers, how they are connected together and other related choices, is debatable. For many teachers, these things will have been done by specialist ICT staff within their schools. There may have been some consultation but often final choices would have come down to issues of procurement or licence. One of the most interesting cases of this type has been the provision of virtual learning environments (VLEs) within schools. Up until very recently, processes of procurement prioritised the use of certain VLEs provided by leading ICT companies, but many teachers found these systems unwieldy and found alternative, sometimes home-made, solutions instead. They made their own choices in spite of the established or received wisdom. However, the vast majority of teachers complied with the decisions made by others within their school or local education authority and lived with the consequences.

So, while teachers' choices about the technological infrastructure within their schools have, on the whole, been decided by others, their area of greatest influence is in matters of curriculum and resources. Here, teachers have a much larger degree of choice about the types of technology to use within a particular unit of work, the uses to which those particular pieces of technology will be put, the time students will spend using that technology and many other matters.

Within the scope of this chapter, it will not be possible to examine all the potential choices that teachers might make. Here, we are going to examine a couple of very common types of technology that are prevalent across all subjects in the secondary school. First, we will examine the Internet as a tool; and, second, we will look at the word processor.

Does the Internet change the way we think?

As we have seen throughout this book already, the Internet is a powerful tool. It has transformed many of the basic tasks that we do every day. From booking cinema tickets to scheduling meetings, updating personal profiles on *Facebook* and sharing key thoughts on *Twitter*, for many of us it is hard to imagine life without it. For us, writing as academics in a large university, the Internet has transformed the way we think, research and teach. From working in schools, we have seen similar transformations. If this is true for us working in employment today, how much more is this the case for our young people who are growing up with this kind of technology around them from an early age?

There are many potential benefits from using the Internet as a learning tool. Research shows that many cognitive skills are substantially enhanced through its use. These include the strengthening of brain functions related to fast-paced problem solving, recognising patterns in a range of data and analysing their important characteristics, and making judgements about the quality of information contained within a particular source. One study of the way that British women searched for information on medical conditions revealed that the speed at which an individual was able to assess the value of a particular page of information increased as they gained familiarity with using the Internet. While an experienced Internet user was able to ascertain the value of a particular page in a few seconds, it took a novice user much longer to find out whether that information was trustworthy or not (Sillence et al. 2007).

Other studies have reported benefits in terms of small increases in our working memory. These increases allow us to become more skilful in juggling ideas, focusing our attention on competing ideas and analysing, almost instantaneously, their relative value. Small and Vorgan report that, for many of us, this has led to our 'developing neural circuitry that is customized for rapid and incisive spurts of direction attention' (2008: 21). Using the Internet also improves a range of lower-level skills, such as hand–eye coordination (through various gaming environments), reflex responses and the processing of visual cues (Green and Bavelier 2003).

Developmental psychologists have explored the effects of different types of media on people's intelligence and learning abilities. The conclusion of Greenfield's recent work (2009) starts with the obvious thought that each medium, each technology, develops a particular aspect of cognitive skill at the expense of others. So, what does she have to say about the Internet? Her research indicates that the growing use of the Internet has led to a 'widespread and sophisticated development of visual-spatial skills'. But what is the trade-off? Greenfield suggests that the new strengths in visual-spatial intelligence go 'hand in hand with a weakening of our capacities for the kind of "deep processing" that underpins mindful knowledge acquisition, inductive analysis, critical thinking, imagination and reflection' (ibid.: 52).

Given findings such as these, writers like Nicholas Carr have argued that, while:

> the Net grants us instant access to a library of information unprecedented in its size and scope, and it makes it easy for us to sort through that library … what the Net diminishes is Johnson's[1] primary kind of knowledge: the ability to know, in depth, a subject for ourselves, to construct within our own minds the rich and idiosyncratic set of connections that give rise to a singular intelligence.

(2010: 143)

Practical task

- Consider how you use the Internet as a resource within your teaching. What do you think are the benefits or limitations of using the Internet? What difference does using the Internet make on how your pupils learn about your subject? How does it make them think about a particular key concept within it, or link together ideas in different ways?

- Think about a specific example from your recent work where you have asked pupils to use the Internet for a particular purpose. What difference would it have made if you had given the information to the pupils in a different way, for example in a textbook or work-sheet? What specific reasons did you have for choosing to use the Internet at that particular moment rather than any alternative tool?

Does a word processor change the way we feel about words?

Our discussion above has briefly considered the Internet and the potential positive or negative effects it has on how we think. There is much more that could be said on that topic. But the key point here was to emphasise that the technologies that we choose to use within our teaching do have consequences on how our pupils understand our subjects as well as how they facilitate particular learning processes within them. Our discussion is going to move on to consider another generic tool that dominates our schools: the word processor.

As writers, the tools we choose to use to write have a major effect on how we feel about words. We are writing this book using a wonderful piece of software called *Scrivener*. *Scrivener* has an increasingly large and loyal following among different groups of writers, including those writing film scripts, plays and, of course, novels and other works of non-fiction. Why do writers choose to use a tool like *Scrivener*? Why not use a standard word processor? The answers are complex, but go to the heart of the relationship between human beings and the tools we use for particular tasks.

Perhaps one of the problems in looking at our current range of technologies and their use within schools is that we are just too close to them to analyse, in an objective way, the impact that they have. The word processor is pervasive. Whether the technology is located within a particular piece of software, or in other locations with keypads or keyboards such as mobile devices, producing text on a screen as opposed to by hand with those other pervasive technologies – the pen or pencil – is becoming the skill of choice for many pupils.

In Chapter 2, we considered the work of Ballard and Doctorow (see pages 19–21). We noted differences in the composition and production processes surrounding their writing of fiction. Looking back even further, similar changes occurred when the typewriter was invented. In a letter of 1916, T. S. Eliot reflected on how he felt the typewriter was changing his ability to write:

> When composing on the typewriter, I find that I am sloughing off all my long sentences which I used to dote upon. Short, staccato, like modern French prose. The typewriter makes for lucidity, but I am not sure that it encourages subtlety.
>
> (Eliot 1988)

Thinking back even further, Carr (2010) recounts the story of the famous philosopher, Friedrich Nietzsche, who, suffering from many ailments that threatened to jeopardise his career as a writer, ordered a typewriter to be delivered to his lodgings in 1882. The Malling-Hansen Writing Ball was an object of great beauty that, with practice, allowed him to write up to 800 characters a minute. It was the fastest typewriter that had been made.

Nietzsche was so delighted with this technology that he composed a short ode to it:

The writing ball is a thing like me: made of iron
Yet easily twisted on journeys.
Patience and tact are required in abundance,
As well as fine fingers, to use us.

But, as Carr reports, the Writing Ball began to have a more subtle effect on Nietzsche's work. His friend, the writer and composer Heinrich Köselitz, began to notice changes in his writing style:

Nietzsche's prose had become tighter, more telegraphic. There was new forcefulness to it, too, as though the machine's power – its 'iron' – was, through some mysterious metaphysical mechanism, being transferred into the words it pressed in the page.

(Carr 2010: 18)

Köselitz's letter to Nietzsche is fascinating. In his own work, he said, his 'thoughts in music and language often depend on the quality of the pen and paper'. Nietzsche replied, 'You are right, our writing equipment takes part in the forming of our thoughts' (Nyíri 1994; Kittler 1999; Cate 2005; Emden 2005).

As we have seen from the examples of T. S. Eliot and Friedrich Nietzsche in this chapter, and the other examples given in Chapter 2, the tools that we choose to use for our writing impose limitations as well as open possibilities. 'We shape our tools' observed John Culkin, 'and thereafter they shape us' (Culkin 1967: 52). Paraphrasing him, we could write that we choose our tools, and thereafter they shape us.

Reflective task

What might be lost if pupils neglect, or forget, the ability to write by hand? Is what is lost compensated for by what is potentially gained through engagement with the modern tools of writing?

The choices that we make, as teachers, in respect of the technologies that we allow into our classrooms, and the ways in which we use these technologies, will fundamentally impact on the processes of teaching and learning that we and our students engage in. So far, we have considered two very common types of technology – the Internet and the word processor – and commented on how their pervasive use may not be as beneficial as might first seem apparent. This is not to say that they are not beneficial and useful as tools for teaching and learning. They are. But a balanced viewpoint, informed by wider historical and cultural analysis, is essential if we are to truly understand the effects they have on how we teach and how our pupils learn.

But the choices we make as teachers are only part of the mix in the modern-day classroom. Our pupils' lives are dominated by choices that they have made in relation to their use of technology for various purposes. Part of our consideration in choosing and using technology within the classroom has to be built upon our understanding of their 'world' of technology. It is to that which our attention now turns.

Understanding the choices that young people make

As writers and educators, we have worked in schools, colleges and universities over the last 20 years. Our interests in and use of technology are wide, diverse, idiosyncratic and constantly evolving. Because we are middle-aged, we very often draw on pre-digital experiences to inform our work with digital technologies. We also try to be open to the experiences of those not working directly in education in order to stimulate our ideas about how best to work with technologies in the classroom. These processes of cross-fertilisation and lateral thinking lie at the heart of our professional practice and have been reflected in the writing of this book. As you engage with our stories, and as we encourage you to reflect on them, we hope you are beginning to establish the contours of your own journey, as teacher and learner in an educational context that is saturated by technology.

Young people make choices. They do so within the economic, social and educational contexts in which they live. To understand how those choices are made let us turn once again to a single story of learning from an earlier age: a personal reflection on the process of learning to play a musical instrument.

Case study 4.1: Reflections on learning to play a musical instrument in the 1970s

I started to learn the piano when I was 5 years old. I remember my first teacher at primary school. I remember the first book that I learnt from (I still have it). I got it out a few weeks ago and flicked through the pieces and exercises. I remember my mother sitting me down at the piano at home and making me practise. 'Little and often, that's the key', she used to say. I enjoyed it. I was probably quite good at it too and made quick progress. By the time I went to high school, aged 11, I had done several examinations and received some certificates. I learnt that these were important stamps of approval.

However, I was also frustrated. Playing the piano was a solitary activity. I was envious of other young musicians I knew who played in orchestras and wind bands in my local area. In the first few weeks of high school I remember going to see the Head of Music and asking if there was another instrument that I could learn to play. He suggested percussion. I'm not sure why. I'd like to think it was because he saw some potential in me. But I think the truth was that he needed a percussionist! Either way, I had weekly percussion lessons and eventually joined the local area youth orchestra.

In both cases, piano and percussion, I learned from regular lessons with a specialist teacher and a collection of tutor books. Apart from these, the piano, my drumsticks, a wooden stool to hit (that was a snare drum) and a collection of cushions (they were the timpani), the tools or technologies in my progression towards becoming a professional musician were simple and straightforward. I played. I hit things. I listened and copied. Later, I learned to perform with others.

Reflective task

Spend a few moments comparing this case study to the processes by which Tom learnt to play the guitar (Chapter 2, pages 25–6). What similarities or differences can you find? Think through the pedagogical as well as the practical consequences of these changes.

Learning a musical instrument is a precise and specialised activity. But the differences in learning to play between 1970 and today reflect more general themes that we have been discussing throughout this book. There are obvious elements such as the collaborative or communal dimensions, of a shared sense of discovery or at least a sharing the journey with others through online tools. The role of the teacher as the single source of authority, while still strong in many musical traditions, has been ameliorated by other sources or systems of support in others. The greater degree of personalisation, of being able to follow one's own interests alongside those of your teacher, is also apparent. Slowing down the performances of the masters (something not easily done on analogue tape machines), micro-analysing technique through high-quality video of close-up performance techniques, and many other features of musical practice can be explored through today's technological tools in ways that were just impossible 40 years ago.

Moving away from musical teaching and learning, there are many more routine activities that young people engage with today through new technologies. Many of these would have been impossible to achieve in previous generations. Perhaps the most ubiquitous pieces of technology in many young people's lives today are social networking websites such as *MySpace* and *Facebook*. As we saw in Chapter 3, these technologies have transformed the ways in which young people represent themselves to the wider world, relate to each other and, more worryingly, can be exploited by others.

Of course, you may wonder how much choice young people have in terms of the technologies and tools they use. The forces of the advertising media are strong and their influence spreads deeply throughout our culture. We hear stories of parents choosing for their children (often negatively because of fears about a particular technology and its use), but how often do we hear stories of young people celebrating the choices they have made? Next time you have the opportunity, why not ask one of your pupils why they use *Facebook* and not *Twitter*? You might be surprised by their answer. Many of our young people can give articulate and passionate accounts of why they have chosen to use the tools they have in their digital portfolio. It may also explain why they find some of the choices that we make, as their teachers, particularly difficult.

Whose choice? Developing our choice of technology in the classroom

This chapter explores the framework of choice in relation to the technologies we use within our teaching. We have argued that these technologies are not neutral in how they impact on the processes of teaching and learning. If we take time to learn how to broaden our understanding of how a particular technology is used, we will notice that it has a range of affordances as well as limitations. We have also considered how the choices that we may make as teachers will coexist alongside choices that young people make in their lives elsewhere. The consequences of their choices of technologies or tools in their wider lives will impact on their ability to work within the formal space of school-based education.

So, what should we be doing to help make informed choices? We would like to suggest a number of practical considerations for your work in this area.

Remember that the choices you make display the particular values that you hold

First, the choices of technology that you include within the classroom are a very real indicator of the values that you hold for your subject, as well as the particular pedagogy that you adopt to teach it. The IWB is an obvious example. Has there ever been a piece of technology that was so inappropriately named? For many teachers, an IWB is nothing more than a twenty-first-century blackboard. Any interactivity can be severely limited by its location in the classroom, a strongly didactic pedagogy and a host of other factors. This is not to say that IWBs should not be used in this way. It is just that the IWB as an object locates itself within the domain of the teacher as 'master' within the classroom. It is often physically located in a space untouchable by pupils, and within the sole control of the teacher. While this is not always the case, the teacher has to be very imaginative and skilful in order to move beyond the strong framing and contextual issues associated with this technology and seek to liberate it from a traditional view of teacher as a presenter of knowledge that pupils need to learn.

Weigh up the pros and cons of individual pieces of technology

Second, before adopting a new piece of technology within your teaching, analyse the pros and cons. We would urge you to consider both. It is often the case with newer technologies that powerful companies are very good at letting you know about the positive, liberating and powerful new features that their technology may contain. If you believe their hype, your teaching will never be the same again should you decide to adopt it! This is never the case. Time and time again throughout this book, we have repeated the message that technology has an important role to play in a twenty-first-century education. There are powerful, meaningful and beneficial uses of a broad range of technologies that we can access in our classrooms. But this needs to be done in a considered and thoughtful way.

Listen to a range of viewpoints

We, as authors, have a range of different experiences with technology and teaching. One of us comes from a school background, one from a college and university background. One of us lectures in social media and new forms of communication, while the other is involved in teacher education. As we have worked together on this book we have both learned much from each other. Can we suggest, gently, that it is important to draw information and ideas from a range of disciplines? Within the world of education, it is easy to listen to the latest educational guru or inspirational speaker. However, in forming judgements about the use of different sorts of technology within your teaching, it will be wise to listen to the voices of the sociologist, the psychologist and the technologist, as well as the educator. While this may seem daunting, it is certainly worthwhile! We would advise you not to become a teacher who just follows the trend. Rather, seek broad counsel about the tools you would like to adopt within your teaching.

Do not become over-reliant on one tool

As a general rule, do not become reliant on one particular type of technology within your teaching. If your pedagogy is broadly speaking a didactic one, you may find it comfortable and helpful to use a presentational technology such as an IWB. This is fine as far as it goes. However, the challenge for you will be to broaden your pedagogical approach where needed and to find tools to help support this development. If you teach the visual arts and you find that your pupils' work is becoming clichéd through the overuse of a particular piece of drawing software, this might be a signal for change. Is uncritical use of the Internet as a research tool yielding poor results in a history project? Perhaps it is time to consider other sources of information retrieval such as textbooks or worksheets where the choice of information is more narrowly focused, or through group discussion where pupils may be able to build on existing knowledge and share this with others.

The examples could be endless and we are sure you will be able to apply this to your own work. You will need to pick the tool to do the job (so do not choose a chisel when a hammer is needed). However, if all you do is hammer all day you will not produce a very good carving!

Maintain your focus on your pedagogy and not the technology

The technology that you choose to use in your teaching will affect you, your subject and your pedagogy. We will focus on the first of these in more detail below. But, as we have seen in respect of our discussion above about the word processor, choosing to use a particular technology affects fundamentally the way in which you and your pupils engage with our particular subject area. This can cause problems. The classically trained musician may find it difficult to find the same level of sensitivity and engagement of sound with an electronic or virtual musical instrument; the geographer may bemoan the lack of map-reading skills in an age of GPS and satellite navigation; the designer may worry about the decline in drawing skills among students being brought up in a world of computer-aided design. In all these examples, and the many that you can consider within your own subject area, technology may be conceived as having a negative influence on skills and understanding. However, as we have emphasised, there will be a range of pros and cons in every case. It is a vital part of our role to consider these carefully and make informed choices.

But, more fundamentally, all aspects of our pedagogy are informed and influenced by the tools that we use. Asking pupils to write an extended piece of writing in their exercise books is not the same as asking them to write it using a word processor. Researching a historical topic on the Internet is not the same as using a textbook; composing a piece of music in an online composition environment is not the same as working with a partner in a practice room. But, more importantly than any of these examples, the actual act of teaching – the words we use, the body language we adopt, the pace of delivery, the sequencing and structuring of lessons, our processes of assessment and evaluation – can all change dramatically as we use different technologies in our classrooms.

The opening of this chapter recounted a story of a chamber orchestra playing with and without chairs. What is a similar analogy within our classrooms? Desks? Computers? What happens when the desks are removed? What happens when we bring computers alongside other resources? What about the physical arrangement of the classroom? Have you tried teaching in a space where pupils sit facing their computer screens with their backs facing you? It is hard. If this is true of physical objects such as desks and chairs, how much more is it the case for tools and technologies that challenge the way we think and feel? This moves us on to our next point.

Do not allow technology to numb your senses

As we have discussed, all technologies impose limitations as well as open up possibilities. Part of the key here is choosing technologies that are appropriate to the tasks at hand and use them skilfully, with full knowledge of both the up- and downsides. The 'numbing' effect of technology has been well documented. Carr, drawing on Marshall McLuhan, writes:

> When we extend some part of ourselves artificially, we also distance ourselves from the amplified part and its natural functions. When the power loom was invented, weavers could manufacture far more cloth during the course of a workday than they'd been able to make by hand, but they sacrificed some of their manual dexterity, not to mention some of their 'feel' for the fabric. Their fingers, in McLuhan's terms, became numb.
>
> (2010: 210)

What is true for the fingers is true for the mind too. Carr goes on to illustrate this by reference to the work of the cartographer. The navigational skills of our ancestors were aided greatly by the invention of the map. It allowed them to travel across lands confidently, and had tremendous benefits in terms of trade and warfare. But this was at a cost. Carr continues:

> Their native ability to comprehend a landscape, to create a richly detailed mental map of their surroundings, weakened. The map's abstract, two-dimensional representation of space interposed itself between the map reader and his perception of the actual land. ... The loss must have had a physical component. When people came to rely on maps rather than their own bearings, they would have experienced a diminishment of the area of their hippocampus devoted to spatial representation. The numbing would have occurred deep in their neurons.
>
> (2010: 211–12)

More recently, neuroscientists have noted a big effect on London taxi drivers' brains as they increasingly rely on GPS devices rather than the traditional process of acquiring 'the knowledge' (Dobson 2006).

Illustrations like these should warn us against being too positive or celebratory about the potential benefits of any one piece of technology. In our experience, while it is often easy to see the potential benefits of bringing a new piece of technology into a classroom, the downsides of any piece of technology, in both physical and cognitive aspects, are often harder to identify and analyse. While this is true for the choices we make in our role as teachers, it is also the case for our young people too. The choices they make about technology in their wider lives may help or hinder their progress as learners within our classrooms. This leads us on to our final point.

Balance teacher and pupil choices

While new technologies are increasingly pervasive in young people's lives, this does not mean that they need to be so within our classrooms. As we have argued, the choice and use of specific pieces of technology within the classroom need to be considered seriously by the teacher, with appropriate deliberation given to the pros and cons of using a particular tool. But it is very easy to be swept along on a tide of technological enthusiasm for all things new. The powerful forces of advertising and marketing target young people throughout their childhood and frame the 'choices' that they make in their technological consumption. Whether it is mobile phones, portable MP3 players, or the latest online role-playing game or social networking site, technology as a form of entertainment, communication and representation has to change rapidly in order to sustain the market.

Within education, things should be different. So, while it is important for teachers to be aware of what is going on outside their schools, it is by no means an automatic assumption that the latest piece of technology is going to be appropriate or desirable for use within the classroom. One area in which this debate has played out in recent years has concerned the use of mobile phones within schools. Sample any selection of schools in your local area and you will find a staggering array of policies about mobile phones and their use. It is not our place to say how mobile phones ought to be used. This is for individual schools to decide. But it is interesting to consider how a very powerful piece of technology is being largely ignored by schools or, at best, limited in terms of pupils' use within school. It is worth asking the question, how would the process of education be different if we truly embraced and explored the potential of this piece of technology and allowed our pupils to use it actively within their lessons? Also, what would be lost?

More generally, the disconnect between young people's extensive use of mobile technologies outside school when compared to their use within school demonstrates an interesting aspect of power in relation to choice. Many schools seem happy to reject the technology itself (i.e. through banning the use of mobile phones in lessons), while completely ignoring the wider cultural, cognitive and neurological effects that having access to these technologies in young people's wider lives has facilitated.

In one sense, the argument is not just about the technology itself and whose choice wins the day. Carr's analysis indicates that the numbing effect of technology leads to alienation:

Alienation is an inevitable by-product of the use of technology. Whenever we use a tool to exert greater control over the outside world, we change our relationship with that world. ... In some cases, alienation is precisely what gives a tool its value. We build houses and sew Gore-Tex jackets because we *want* to be alienated from the wind and the rain and the cold. ... An honest appraisal of any new technology, or of progress in general, requires a sensitivity to what's lost as well as what's gained. We shouldn't allow the glories of technology to blind our inner watchdog to the possibility that we've numbed an essential part of our self.

(2010: 212)

How has the mobile phone changed the way in which young people relate to the world? What has been gained, and what has been lost? And what happens when that tool is taken away? Will pupils be able to regain any potential sensitivity that has been lost?

As teachers, whether the choice of a piece of technology comes from our own understanding, or whether it relates to a technology that is situated in the wider lives of young people, it is essential that our analysis of that tool and its use for educational purposes is carried out rigorously and conscientiously.

Practical task

Choose a piece of technology that you use regularly in your subject teaching. Work through each of the seven points above and apply them to your use of this technology. To what extent has your use of this technology been informed by a critical analysis? If it hasn't, what reasons did you have for adopting the tool in the first place? Having completed your analysis here, what has it revealed?

Summary

As participants in a media revolution we have all, teachers and students alike, embraced new technologies. That those technologies shape us and our practices as teachers and learners is clear. How they do so, and what the end point may be, is less clear.

We have argued in this chapter that, while we cannot resist the digital, we can begin to articulate a framework that can enable us to make informed and appropriate choices about what, how and when particular tools are adopted. We have also suggested that a more nuanced response is needed that goes beyond the 'use it' or 'ban it' reaction to the new. For any technology (including the chairs that we began the chapter exploring), we need to understand what the affordances of a particular tool are (what it is natively good at doing), what its limitations are, and what might be lost if it is adopted. Only after having explored these questions can we begin to make informed, contextual choices about which tools can have a valuable impact on the processes of teaching and learning that we and our students engage in.

With this framework and the questions that emerge from it in place, we move in our next chapter to consider the potential of social media to enhance, excite and extend creativity and creative thinking in our classrooms.

Discussion points

- How can specific pieces of technology help support my role as a teacher?
- How can specific pieces of technology help support my role as a learner?
- To what extent could I adopt technologies that pupils are familiar with in my classroom? How would pupils feel about this if I did?
- What is lost when I bring digital technologies into the classroom space?

Useful websites/resources

www.downes.ca Stephen Downes's website, *Stephen's Web*, described as 'a digital research laboratory for innovation in the use of online media in education'.

www.futurelab.org.uk/resources/curriculum-development-and-youth-media *Futurelab*, Curriculum Development and Youth Media web page.

Note

1 Samuel Johnson famously argued that there were two kinds of knowledge: knowing something and knowing where to find out about something.

References

Carr, N. G. (2010) *The Shallows: What the Internet is doing to our brains*, New York: W.W. Norton.

Cate, C. (2005) *Friedrich Nietzsche*, Woodstock, NY: Overlook Press.

Culkin, J. (1967) 'A schoolman's guide to Marshall McLuhan', *The Saturday Review*, March 18: 51–3 and 70–2.

Dobson, J. (2006) 'Taxi drivers' knowledge helps their brains grow', *The Independent*, 17 December.

Eliot, V. (ed.) (1988) *The Letters of T. S. Eliot 1898–1992*, New York: Harcourt Brace.

Emden, C. (2005) *Nietzsche on Language, Consciousness, and the Body*, Urbana, IL: University of Illinois Press.

Furedi, F. (2009) *Wasted : Why education isn't educating*, London: Continuum.

Green, C. S. and Bavelier, D. (2003) 'Action video game modifies visual selective attention', *Nature*, 423: 534–7.

Greenfield, P. M. (2009) 'Technology and informal education: what is taught, what is learned', *Science*, 323(5910): 69–71.

Kittler, F. A. (1999) *Gramophone, Film, Typewriter*, Stanford, CA: Stanford University Press.

Nyíri, J. C. (1994) 'Thinking with a word processor', in Casati, R. (ed.) *Philosophy and the Cognitive Sciences*, Vienna: Hölder-Pichler-Tempsky.

Selwyn, N. (2010) 'Looking beyond learning: notes towards the critical study of educational technology', *Journal of Computer Assisted Learning*, 26: 65–73.

Sillence, E., Briggs, P., Harris, P. R. and Fishwick, L. (2007) 'How do patients evaluate and make use of online health information?', *Social Science and Medicine*, 64: 1853–62.

Small, G. W. and Vorgan, G. (2008) *iBrain: Surviving the technological alteration of the modern mind*, New York: Collins Living.

5

Making, sharing and connecting with digital networked technologies

Key questions

- What does it mean to be creative in a connected world and how can digital networked technologies help us as teachers?

- How can the notion of creativity be redefined as a collaborative element in the educational use of digital networked technologies?

- How can processes of making, sharing and connecting help develop my subject pedagogy?

The previous chapter examined the issues surrounding the choice and use of pieces of technology within educational settings. It argued for an increased analysis and investigation of the affordances and limitations of digital tools within the processes of teaching and learning. Teachers face a barrage of claims for the positive effects that such tools can offer. While many of these may be justified, there needs to be a calmer, more systematic approach. The education of young people is too important.

As Arendt writes:

> Education is the point at which we decide whether we love the world enough to assume responsibility for it and by the same token save it from ruin which, except for renewal, except for the coming of the new and young, would be inevitable. And education, too, is where we decide whether we love our children enough not to expel them from our world and leave them to their own devices, nor to strike from their hands their chance of undertaking something new, something unforeseen by us, but to prepare them in advance for the task of renewing a common world.
>
> (1961: 196)

Arendt's words are as relevant today as they were in 1961. Note the responsibility placed on our role as teachers to make decisions on behalf of our pupils and to make these decisions based on our care for them. While experiments such as the Hole-in-the-Wall project recounted in Chapter 1 (see pages 7–9) provide a fascinating insight into what happens when young people are given freedom to organise themselves and their learning, even in this project the 'teacher' had made decisions that affected how these young people were able to access and work with ideas. Central to Arendt's thesis is the notion that we, as teachers, have access to knowledge and ideas that our pupils do not have and that we know something about the best way to introduce these things. However, also notice that she suggests that there are things that are, as yet, unforeseen by our pupils and ourselves. We cannot predict the futures that they will face, the new jobs and opportunities their futures might contain, or the types of practical skills or understanding they will need to succeed. However, we do know, Arendt says, that we can prepare them for those future tasks through a careful exemplification and study of the world as it is today. She argued that pupils are best prepared for their future lives by teachers who educate them to understand the world that we know. Or, in Furedi's words, 'there is a need to preserve the past for the sake of the new' (2009: 42). Part of this process will require us to be actively involved in exploring the world of social media, the key focus of this chapter.

These thoughts have interesting parallels with the themes of this book, which focus on digital technologies and their application within teaching and learning. First, for many, technology is explicitly linked to the new. We might suggest, from Arendt's perspective, that becoming overly preoccupied with the new is a dangerous position for educators. Second, Arendt highly values the knowledge that we have as adults and suggests that we, as teachers, should value this and use it wisely. While young people are curious about technology and quick to use it in new and imaginative ways, there is no automatic reason why this should cause us to embrace their new approaches and use them within formal education. There may be good reasons for doing so, but there may be even better reasons for holding back on occasions.

Reflective task

The increasing availability of hardware and software at reasonable prices has empowered teachers and young people to work with technology in ways unimaginable a few years ago. This has had a huge impact on the content of the various curriculum areas and, with equal force, demanded that teachers reconsider their subject pedagogy as these new technologies become common teaching and learning tools.

Think about recent experiences in your own teaching practice. These could be related to observations you have done or lessons you have taught yourself. Have you seen:

- any examples of technologies being used in imaginative ways to inspire students' learning?
- lessons being taught that could not have been delivered without the use of a particular piece of ICT?
- examples of teachers developing their pedagogy as they bring old or new technologies into the classroom environment?
- what we might call creative teaching or learning inspired by or through the use of ICT in the classroom?

Creativity

The use of ICT in education is not the only field in which rhetoric abounds. New notions of 'creativity' and 'critical thinking' have dominated many education discourses in recent years too. This chapter will consider some of these ideas and discuss the use of social media and the potential benefits they can bring. But before we do that, it will be worth restating some key ideas drawn from the debate about creativity within schooling.

Creativity involves creation. At one level, this can seem like a magical or mysterious process, especially if one's view of creativity is based on notions of creating something out of nothing. For example, Boden writes:

> If we take seriously the dictionary definition of creation, to 'bring into being or form out of nothing', creativity seems to be not only unintelligible, but strictly impossible. No craftsman or engineer ever made an artefact from nothing. And sorcerers (or their apprentices) who conjure broom and buckets out of this air do so not by any intelligible means, but by occult wizardry. The 'explanation' of creativity thus reduces to either denial or magic.
>
> (1990: 2)

As we shall see, this 'Harry Potter' view of creativity is extremely unhelpful. For many writers, creativity has been described as a *process* that is situated within a specific *domain*. Both these features, process and domain, contextualise creativity in a more helpful way for educators. However, the majority of the literature contextualises creativity within the remit of the individual. As we go on to see, this can limit our approach to creativity with social media in unhelpful ways.

Creativity is a process

Early models of creativity were constituted by various stages of action or thought. In Wallas's early model (1926) there were four stages: preparation, incubation, illumination and verification. In the preparation phase, consideration was given to a particular issue; the incubation phase represented a time where new thoughts and considerations emerged; the illumination phase concerned the emergence of a solution; and the verification phase involved some kind of testing of that solution.

This creative process involves the mind and the body. In obvious expressions of creativity, such as within dance for example, the twin aspects of body and mind are clear. But even within more abstract or theoretical dimensions of creativity, such as dealing with mathematical processes, the mind and body are equally involved. The use of symbols, external tools or technologies and other elements all demonstrate that creativity is not solely something that happens within our heads.

The creative process contains many dimensions. One key process relates to decision-making. Divergent thinking, namely thinking 'outside the box', emphasises unusual decisions that can lead to something extraordinary taking place. Often divergent thinking occurs as a result of existing patterns of thought, or process, being challenged, extended or overturned in some way.

Many would argue that everyone has the capacity for creative thought and action. Boden's work defines different outcomes of the creative process as either 'P-creative' or 'H-creative'. P-creative outcomes are *psychological*, and have meaning and importance for the individual involved; H-creative outcomes are *historically* important, that is, no one has had that idea before (Boden 1990: 32). Craft puts a different set of terminology together to describe a similar thing. Her definition of the P-creative process is 'the kind of creativity which guides choices and route-finding in everyday life, or what I have come to term "little c" creativity' (2000: 3).

Creativity is situated within domains

Creativity is situated within a domain, a context of some sort. It is never decontextualised. For Csikszentmihalyi, creativity could only occur when there is an interplay between an individual agent and a specific domain. He defined a 'domain' as a 'set of symbolic rules and procedures' contained within a field such as mathematics, gastronomy or music (1996: 26). In another chapter, he continues:

For creativity to occur, a set of rules and practices must be transmitted from the domain to the individual. The individual must then produce a novel variation in the content of the domain. The domain then must be selected by the field for inclusion in the domain.

(ibid.: 315)

This notion of 'inclusion' is interesting because it moves us away from the individual, as the centre of the creative process, and brings in the concept of creativity, and the outputs of the creative process, being about a relationship between different individuals within specific domains. Csikszentmihalyi calls these people 'gatekeepers' who have to decide 'whether a new idea or product should be included in the domain' (ibid.: 28). Bringing these ideas together, Csikszentmihalyi noted that:

One can be a creative carpenter, cook, composer, chemist, or clergyman, because the domains of woodworking, gastronomy, music, chemistry, and religion exist and one can evaluate performance by reference to their traditions.

(ibid.: 315)

As we will explore below, these ideas are also far from unproblematic in the context of new definitions of creativity inspired by social media.

Creativity has certain characteristics

Within these broad definitions of creativity as a process situated within domains, we can see how creativity becomes something that is situated within all fields of human endeavour. While the school curriculum may contain some areas that seem more creative than others (e.g. the Arts), it is important to resist the temptation to think of creativity as being someone else's job! The National Curriculum and other materials have made this point time and time again over the last 15 years. For example, in 1999 the *National Curriculum Handbook* stated that:

By providing rich and varied contexts for pupils to acquire, develop and apply a broad range of knowledge, understanding and skills, the curriculum should enable pupils to think creatively and critically, to solve problems and to make a difference for the better. It should give them the opportunity to become creative, innovative, enterprising and capable of leadership to equip them for their future lives as workers and citizens.

(QCA 1999: 11–12)

The most recent National Curriculum framework (QCDA 2008) outlines how every subject within the secondary curriculum should explore the concept of creativity through the various Key Concepts and Key Processes.

In summary, we can glean the following key points about creativity as developed within the educational literature. First, it involves mental and physical processes; it is situated within domains and it is characterised by various activities and characteristics. Chief among these are the notions of imagination and purposeful behaviour that lead to originality (within an individual's life experience, 'small c' creativity in Craft's terms or P-creative outcomes in Boden's analysis).

This brief overview of some of the key concepts associated with creativity within education sets the scene for this chapter, which is examining how digital networked technologies help develop new approaches to making, sharing and connecting in our teaching. However, the existing literature on creativity in education does, on the whole, situate creativity within the context and experience of the individual pupil. As we will now go on to examine, this model of creativity as solely an individual process needs to be challenged. Young people today grow up in a connected world. Creativity needs to be re-examined in a setting of collaboration through social media.

Creativity in a connected world

As we discussed above, within the world of education creativity is often conceived as being an attribute of an individual pupil. Although we have seen that creativity is an active mental and physical process, with certain characteristics and situated within specific domains, the vast majority of the educational literature has not examined how these facets of creativity apply to, and are expanded within, a world connected by social media.

To illustrate this point, we asked three professionals in various fields to reflect on their working practices. Each professional – an independent computer game developer, a composer and a visual artist – would describe various elements of their work as 'creative'. These are their reflections.

Computer game developer

I work as an independent games developer. Within this field, there is a well-established online culture of cooperation and collaboration, together with a strong sense of community. This community is self-supporting at a number of levels. For new members, there is a wealth of freely available tutorials, ranging from introductory guides suitable for people with no programming experience to materials covering advanced programming topics. People are keen to provide assistance and advice. Many developers share example source codes and discuss algorithms and techniques, as opposed to keeping their methods secret, and also provide free software and tools, such as *sfxr* (sound effects generator), *PXTone* (music production tool), *Flixel* and *FlashPunk* (frameworks for 2D Flash-based games). Other users produce instructional information regarding these tools, such as video how-to guides on *YouTube*.

In terms of collaboration, programmers share their assets (pieces of code, editing mechanisms and other stuff) on a regular basis. They form ad hoc teams to work on particular products and give feedback and constructive criticism on each other's work. Through forums, we also discuss all the theoretical and conceptual elements of game design, including ideas about story writing, content creation and game-play mechanics.

I particularly like attending events such as contests or game jams. These give you an opportunity to meet with people and explore new game-play and design ideas. For example, we might meet in a physical location (perhaps a cyber-café) and work on a particular project together over a 48-hour period. Trying to produce a complete game in such a short time can help focus the mind! Also, most of our collaborative work is done through online spaces, so it is nice to meet a few 'real' people; and seeing how other developers work can be quite inspirational.

Composer

When I tell people that I'm a composer I get an interesting response. Many think I spend hours crouching over manuscript paper and pencil, lit by candlelight! Nothing could be further from the truth. In fact, I'm not that good at reading music (the notated type) at all. Most of my work is done in my home studio. I make extensive use of various bits of music technology, including hardware such as a mixing desk, synths and drum machines. I also use quite a bit of software. Some of these are commercial packages. Other bits I've worked on myself and developed under Creative Commons licensing frameworks.

Most of my composition work is done to a particular brief that I get from a client. It's important for me to understand the brief correctly, but it is only the starting point of my composition work. I need to get inspiration from other sources. This is where I rely on being connected to the outside world (it can be lonely in the studio). I use the Internet to explore images, bits of films, stories and sometimes music. I go on different bulletin boards (often nothing to do with music) to chat with other people about what I've found and get their perspectives on things.

At the early stage of my composition work, I might share some of my initial ideas online using file-sharing and specific websites that allow you to upload your tracks and receive feedback. I can't do this with final compositions due to the commercial nature of my work. But I find it really helpful to share random musical ideas within a wider community. I don't think it is because I need reassurance about my work. I've done this for quite a while and I feel confident about my own abilities as a composer. It's more about using others as a spark for new ideas and directions for my work. It's easy to get stuck in a rut or a particular way of developing ideas. I need to draw on different sources for my initial inspiration and then sustain that inspiration fix through the creative process too. Others online help me do that by providing challenge (a bit of 'grit' in the creative process perhaps?). I hope I return the favour for them too.

Digital animator

One recent example from my work related to the planning and preparation of a group exhibition. A logo for the group, and other publicity materials, were all designed and amended without anyone having to travel, therefore costs associated with a group of this nature were lower and time spent travelling between locations was kept to a minimum. The exhibition itself was all planned online. Artists submitted their work online too, with only one initial face-to-face meeting to establish the themes. The layout of the exhibition space and exhibits was mocked up using *Google's Sketch Up*, with artists' work being clearly incorporated in the virtual environment. This model was shared among all participants, the funders as well as the individual artists, which gave everyone involved a clear idea of what the exhibition space would look like and how it would work.

Facebook is an excellent vehicle for publishing events. Each person involved could send out invitations and publicity materials to their individual networks. This also gave the group a good idea of how many people would be attending the private view, which helped make decisions on what amount of refreshments to supply. Everything was organised through these applications, even down to a timetable for invigilators. The project ran without a hitch and I certainly would use this method for a collaborative event in the future.

Online resources such as *DropBox* and *Facebook* have been extremely useful in a number of collaborative art projects. *DropBox* enables a group to share files instantly from their computer's desktop. Any type of file can be shared quickly and easily among the group, and *Word* documents, schedules, photographs, videos and image files appear in a folder like any other on your system. It is particularly useful when artists in the group live in different locations or countries. *DropBox* enables the group to feel connected and have instant input to the development of ideas.

Reflective task

What did you make of these three reflections? Did anything surprise you? What did you learn? Where does the notion of creativity fit within a connected world? Is teaching a solitary or a collaborative exercise?

What about your work as a teacher? How did you answer the question in the reflective task above? Is teaching a solitary or a collaborative exercise? How does this idea of creativity in a collaborative, connected way impact on it? How could the use of digital networked technologies begin to impact on your work and allow you to develop an alternative approach to what you currently do? Perhaps, for many of you, teaching is both a solitary and a collaborative activity. While you are working with young people every day (and this, after all, is highly collaborative!), you may also feel isolated and disconnected professionally. Teachers often express this viewpoint when we have asked them about it. You may spend a large proportion of your time in a classroom and seldom have the opportunity to discuss issues with other colleagues. Over time, this can lead to a sense of marginalisation and disengagement, of doing the same thing over and over again, and a distinct lack of creativity in terms of your subject, its presence within your classroom and its place within your own pedagogy.

For all these reasons (and probably a lot more), we believe that it is important to think about creativity beyond the individual. What does it mean to be creative in a connected world and how can digital networked technologies help us as teachers? Moving from a position in which creativity has been dominated by the 'individual' mind or body, today, in the experiences of many working across a huge range of contexts, creativity is something that is collaborative and communal, not easily reduced to internalised, individual cognitive processes. Fortunately for us, there are many writers who have begun to explore this very point in their own, different ways. As we consider some of their work, it will be important to apply their ideas to your own work as a teacher. The practical and reflective tasks are designed to help you do this.

Making is connecting: expanding our vision for creativity

David Gauntlett's recent book (2011) is a fascinating read. This section of our book takes its title (*Making is Connecting*) and applies it to our thinking about how we, as teachers, and our students share and develop creativity through technology. Gauntlett takes a historical perspective on creativity and argues that it has always been about connecting people. While he recognises that many writers and thinkers have located creativity within the context of the individual human mind and its capacity to think and develop new thoughts (e.g. with Csikszentmihalyi's work as we described on page 81), his broader analysis of what creativity is ties up with the concept of making. So, early in his book, he argues that creative people engage in making, but that this making is in fact part of the same process of connecting with others. How? He summarises it in three ways:

Making is connecting because you have to connect things together (materials, ideas or both) to make something new.

Making is connecting because acts of creativity usually involve, at some point, a social dimension and connect us with other people.

And making is connecting because through making things and sharing them in the world, we increase our engagement and communication with our social and physical environments.

(Gauntlett 2011: 2)

Gauntlett's focus on the process of creativity, expressed through making with its integral element of connecting, leads him to a very different definition for creativity compared to those we considered in the earlier part of this chapter. Here, he focuses, perhaps unsurprisingly, on the everyday process of creativity that combines making and connecting in an integral manner. But he also focuses on the feelings that arise when one is involved in a creative process:

> Everyday creativity refers to a process that brings together at least one active human mind, and the material or digital world, in the activity of making something. The activity has not been done in this way by this person (or these people) before. The process may arouse various emotions, such as excitement and frustration, but most especially a feeling of joy. When witnessing and appreciating the output, people may sense the presence of the maker, and recognise those feelings.

(ibid.: 76)

In a very obvious and simple sense, teachers are engaged in making things. Following Gauntlett's thesis, if we are involved in making things then we are involved in connecting with things too.

So far in this chapter, we have surveyed some of the basic definitions and interpretations of creativity in education. Generally, these define creativity as a process, situated within particular domains and with various characteristics. However, they prioritise and emphasise creativity as an individual attribute – something that teachers or pupils either have, or do not have, but that can be developed. In this section we have explored how creativity has a collaborative and connected dimension. For some (Gauntlett 2011), there is a historical narrative to this assertion. For others (as in our case studies about the work of an independent computer game developer, a composer and a digital animator), a connected and collaborative process of working within a specific field is a key element in the development of their own creativity and, more than that, there is a willingness to work together, share ideas and offer constructive feedback and criticism in pursuit of joint creative endeavours.

It is time to turn our attention, more explicitly, to the role that networked digital technologies or social media can play in this. What examples are there of creativity being encouraged through this connected and collaborative world? And what can we learn from these examples as we seek to develop ourselves as teachers? As we have seen, our process of curriculum development is explicitly tied to our ongoing professional development.

New media, sharing and creativity

Authors such as Gauntlett (2011) and Shirky (2008, 2010) present numerous examples in their writings of how new media have been utilised to bring people together to collaborate and share, creatively, on various projects for public benefit. We are not proposing to replicate these stories in detail here. However, it is interesting to consider their analysis of common Web 2.0 applications or frameworks that have found their way into educational settings.

So, briefly, we will consider a few of these below. We have chosen the following five examples because they are all focused around sharing and making something with others using social media. We will consider the implications of these five examples for our work as teachers in the following section.

Wikipedia: sharing knowledge

For some, *Wikipedia* has never been taken seriously. As writers who work in a university, we have often heard *Wikipedia* derided by fellow academics and dismissed as an improper source for academic discourse or citation. This is unfortunate. What is your school's view on *Wikipedia*? Do you encourage your students to use it? Do you, or they, contribute to it?

Shirky calculates that the total amount of time spent creating *Wikipedia* (and this includes the writing of original articles and the edits that people make to these articles) is 'one hundred million hours' (2010: 10). This sounds like (and is) a massive amount of human thought and time. But how does it compare to other activities? Well, Shirky also calculates that Americans watch roughly two hundred *billion* hours of television every year (i.e. enough time for 200 *Wikipedia* projects to be constructed). The process by which *Wikipedia* has been constructed is analysed in his earlier book (Shirky 2008). He gives the example of an article about asphalt. First of all, someone, somewhere, decided that an article on asphalt was required. They created it. This actually happened in 2001 and the original article said, 'Asphalt is a material used for road coverings' (ibid.: 118–19).

Once that article existed, other people read it. Eventually, a self-selecting group of readers became editors of that article. They made changes, added helpful information, and fixed typos and grammatical errors. They could have also made mistakes, included inaccurate information or made the article less comprehensible. But this did not matter. Why? A *Wikipedia* article is conceived as a process not a product. It is never finished or published in that sense. As Shirky states:

> For a *Wikipedia* article to improve, the good edits simply have to outweigh the bad ones. Rather than filtering contributions before they appear in public, *Wikipedia* assumes that new errors will be introduced less frequently than existing ones will be corrected. This assumption has proven correct; despite occasional vandalism, *Wikipedia* articles get better, on average, over time.
>
> (ibid.: 119)

In Shirky's example of an article on asphalt, by 2007 129 different contributors had added their work within the article. By then, it had subdivided into an article on asphalt as a petroleum derivative, and another on asphalt as a road covering. Numerous details about the chemistry, history, geographical distribution of asphalt deposits and even the etymology of the word itself had been added and edited by the *Wikipedia* community.

What is the success of *Wikipedia* based on? How has it managed to be so successful in getting people involved in writing, for free, about its huge range of subjects. First, all contributors are free agents. They are not employees. They can choose when to work, how to work, what to work on or whether to work at all. There is a happy blend of energetic workers and occasional contributors who exist side by side.

Second, there is a freedom for all to contribute regardless of their skills, ability or knowledge. All can participate. Anyone can start an article on anything, regardless of their level of knowledge. In fact, the very inadequacy of detail within a particular article will inspire others to take it on and improve it; 'many more people are willing to make a bad article better than are willing to start a good article from scratch' (ibid.: 122). Shirky relates this to the process by which a coral reef is formed over many years. The key to this action is to give as much freedom as possible to the potential contributor.

Finally, *Wikipedia* makes it as easy as possible to contribute to the project. It values even the smallest of contributions and provides simple access for those who want to contribute:

> By making the size of the smallest possible contribution very small, and by making the threshold for making that change small as well, *Wikipedia* maximises contributions across an enormous range of participation. This wouldn't have worked when amateur participation was limited, but it works remarkably well when the participant pool can be drawn from the whole world.
>
> (ibid.: 200)

Facebook: sharing oneself

If *Wikipedia* is an example of collaboration and creativity in respect of knowledge, *Facebook* is perhaps the ultimate form of personal sharing. For many of us, and our pupils, *Facebook* is the primary site for the presentation of our virtual self to the world. For many, *Facebook* has made it easier for people to express themselves online and communicate aspects of their identity to the wider world.

However, it can do much more than that. Shirky recounts the story of HSBC deciding to revoke its policy of interest-free overdrafts for students and recent graduates. Within weeks, a Cambridge University student had set up a site called 'Stop the Great HSBC Graduate Rip-Off!' and within days thousands of students had signed up. Shirky continues:

> Critically, *Facebook* was the one place where both current students and recent graduates could all be reached together; in years past, the dispersal of the graduates made it hard to communicate with them, but now they remain part of the social fabric of a college even after dispersing physically. *Facebook* also helped lower the switching costs, as current and former students began

researching and recommending other UK banks that still offered interest-free overdrafts.

(ibid.: 180)

Eventually, HSBC caved in, but not because its customers were unhappy; it was because its customers were unhappy and coordinated.

There is a massive amount that could be written about *Facebook* and its ability to allow its users to communicate and collaborate. But our focus here is on how sharing, making and connecting lead to new forms of connection and creative thought. In this sense, it is interesting to read Shirky's analysis of a progression in sharing from what might be called a base level of personal sharing (such as that found by your average *Facebook* user), to other, perhaps more creative, activities. In his words, 'the organisation of sharing has many forms'. In his model, there are four main 'levels':

> One such form is personal sharing, done among otherwise uncoordinated individuals; ... Another, more involved form, is communal sharing, which takes place inside a group of collaborators; ... Then there is public sharing, when a group of collaborators actively wants to create a public resource; ... Finally, civic sharing is when a group is actively trying to transform society.
>
> (ibid.: 173)

There are some very obvious implications of this for our work as educators that we will consider further below.

Ushahidi: sharing values

Ushahidi is the Swahili word for 'testimony'. As a form of social media, it was first developed in early 2008 to help citizens in Kenya track the numerous outbreaks of ethnic violence following elections. Since then, it has been used on numerous occasions to help track information in the aftermath of natural disasters, such as the Haiti earthquake or Queensland's floods. *Ushahidi* provides a technological platform that allows anyone with access to text messaging, email, *Twitter* or the Web to share information in almost real time about what is happening in their particular location. This concept of crowd-sourcing is very powerful. The citizen journalism that it facilitates has changed the way in which information is reported and shared.

Ushahidi is a fantastic example of civic sharing. It was created and built on open-source software, free for anyone to develop and use. It makes use of cheap and flexible tools such as mobile phones. It builds on people's desire to do something positive for the world and, perhaps most importantly, it shows that 'once you've figured out how to tap the surplus [in Shirky's argument, this equates to the increased amount of leisure time that many people around the world enjoy] in a way that people care about, others can replicate your technique, over and over, around the world' (ibid.: 17).

YouTube: sharing images

As we are sure you know, *YouTube* is the world's largest video-sharing site. Since its launch in 2005, it has dominated online video, serving up a staggering one billion videos every day since 2009. In Gauntlett's exposition on *YouTube* and its influence (2011), he situates *YouTube* within his metaphor of Web 2.0 as an allotment garden. Each item, each video, is a self-contained package that other users cannot easily edit or add to. In that sense, he says, it is like adding an additional plant into a communal allotment. However, he continues:

> Those items can be nurtured by others (through ratings and links) and responded to (through comments and further videos). Contributing diverse plants to a shared garden is a perfectly good form of collaboration: we don't actually need to be pruning, feeding, and fussing over bits of individual plants together. So it's still a Web 2.0 community, but with the level of mashability being set one notch higher.
>
> (ibid.: 84)

Gauntlett goes on to explore how *YouTube* is the archetype for digital creative platforms. It provides a framework for mass participation and is pretty much agnostic about the content that is housed within it. It also seeks to generate and foster a sense of community in various ways, notably by encouraging everyone to participate regardless of skill or expertise (e.g. in terms of camera work, or editing) or content. This has led Burgess and Green to comment that:

> However charming or frivolous the content of their videos might be, what all the entrepreneurial *YouTube* stars have in common is the fit between their creative practice and the dynamics of *YouTube* as a platform for participatory culture.
>
> (2009: 105)

Script Frenzy: sharing stories

Each year, for the last five years, *Script Frenzy* has run a month-long competition for writers. Last year, 21,008 amateur writers volunteered to write at least 100 pages of text, resulting in a staggering 363,906 submitted pages of writing. *Script Frenzy* charges no fee to participate and there are no valuable prizes awarded or best scripts singled out. Every writer who completes the goal of 100 pages receives a handsome *Script Frenzy* Winner's Certificate and a Web icon.

Script Frenzy is a very good example of a self-regulating platform for writers. One of the frequently asked questions on their website is 'Couldn't someone just write the same sentence for 100 pages and say they won?', to which the good-humoured response is:

> Technically, yes. And there are always one or two people who do. But they spend the rest of their summer haunted by the knowledge that instead of simply

writing a script, they chose to bamboozle the community. Typically these folks are tormented for life; sometimes they go on to run Hollywood studios.

(*Script Frenzy* 2011)

As with many social networking sites, *Script Frenzy* utilises a very low bar for participation because it knows that the vast majority of participants will not bother to abuse the platform. It does not even keep the scripts for others to read. Once a script has been submitted and verified against the 100-page check, it is deleted. However, writers can choose to share an extract of their work on the site should they wish to.

The obvious question about *Script Frenzy* is why have increasing numbers of people, year on year, been bothered to write and submit 100 pages of original text in order to receive a virtual certificate and Web icon?

Developing your use of digital networked technologies

Learning to teach creatively with new media involves an active decision, made by you, to do things in a different way. There are many basic things that might change. Involving your pupils in active learning, or activity-based learning, may well be a key to teaching creatively. Bringing more real-world examples into the classroom for pupils to engage with and solve problems around, or discuss key ideas through, may also be teaching creatively. But, as we explored throughout the previous chapter, just adopting pieces of technology within your teaching will not result in you becoming a creative teacher, or your pupils becoming creative learners. Pieces of technology are just tools. They are not the sole answer to inspiring and capturing imaginations. Their novelty only lasts for a while.

The five illustrations of new media that we discussed above were chosen for a particular reason. They each illustrate, in different ways, key aspects of new media that help participants make, connect and create in new ways. Before you read on, spend a few minutes thinking about the following questions.

Reflective task

Take each of the five examples explored above in turn. For each one, consider what key elements of the new media might inform:

- the way in which you organise the activities that take place within your classroom;
- the broader pedagogy that you are seeking to develop within your teaching.

In reflecting on this task, we hope that you began to see some of the implications of these new social media for how you might organise your own classroom environment, the tools that you use within it and the spaces, whether physical, conceptual or virtual (or a mixture of all three), that you open up for pupils to explore ideas within. So, what are the implications for the development of a pedagogy that embraces the making, sharing and connecting aspects of new media?

The power of the social experience

One of the key aspects from our perspective is the relation between an individual participant and the group with social media. So, for example, *Wikipedia* as an example of a social medium that is involved in sharing knowledge teaches us several things. First, it is focused on collaboration and knows that content is produced as a result of the interactions that occur between individual participants. This affects the choice of content as well as the content itself.

Second, it is not overly concerned with the mistakes because it knows, on average, that the mistake of an individual will be picked up and corrected by others within the group. On balance, good and accurate levels of knowledge are produced and shared through this process.

Third, did you note the emphasis on process not product? No *Wikipedia* article is ever finished, it is always a work in progress and should be read as such. This provisionality in reading and understanding knowledge is vital. It relates to other sources of knowledge too. Just because something is in print, it does not mean that it should be accepted as truth. It needs to be taken, contextualised, analysed and reflected on. With *Wikipedia*, unlike textbooks or other encyclopaedias, you have the opportunity to contribute something back to the article itself should you want to expand on something, contend with a statement, correct an inaccuracy, or whatever.

This relationship between the individual and group also comes across strongly in the example of sharing information or data, such as in *Ushahidi*. Here, the crowd-sourcing principle only works because of the aggregation of small pieces of data focused on a particular event (e.g. a natural disaster or election). But, in a similar way to the *Wikipedia* example, the small contributions of many individuals lead to something that is worth much more than its individual parts.

Many teachers have explored the use of *Wikipedia* within their work. The key benefit is that it provides a collaborative way of working in subjects that are often dominated by individual approaches. So, whether it is writing a poem, a film script or a play, using a 'wiki' approach will help your pupils work together. Similarly, collaborative approaches to art or music-making can be facilitated through shared work spaces (online or offline) that draw on these principles. The challenge for us as teachers may be related to processes of assessment as much as anything else.

If access is easy, growth will follow

The second key point about a pedagogy that embraces the making, sharing and connecting aspects of new media is that it will make the level of access to a particular set of ideas, or subject, easy for all to access. There should be no stumbling blocks or complexities at that first point of engagement. Teachers will need to be skilful and imaginative in designing new 'doorways' into their subject areas. Rather than requiring several keys, strong fingers to unlock bolts or a swipe card, these doorways need to swing open smoothly and easily for the enquiring mind.

Many subjects contain complicated ideas. They require, or demand, an intellectual struggle of engagement at particular points. The process of introducing young people to these big ideas is what is at stake here. To use the illustration of *Wikipedia*, do not demand a finished article from your pupils at the outset of their journey with you into a particular topic or concept. Rather, embrace the tentative ideas that are put forward, allow them to be nurtured in various ways and that seed of engagement will grow over time.

One science teacher I worked with found this concept challenging. Rightly, perhaps, his view was that his subject contained complicated ideas that, if 'watered down', reduced their value in the minds of his pupils and, correspondingly, led to a reduced sense of engagement. Over time, as we worked together, he began to see that it was not about the content as such; rather, it was the process of introducing pupils to that content that was at stake. Through considering and anticipating the journey towards his subject's 'big ideas', this teacher was able to map out potential way-points for his pupils and celebrate with them their progress over a number of lessons. What was the case for this science teacher is also true for many other subjects. In music, for example, certain musical styles may be considered remote from pupils' general musical listening habits. However, with skill and care, even the most remote musical styles can be introduced to young people and learned to be appreciated over time. Engagement in a subject can be built, and it need not require knowledge to be reduced to its lowest common denominator.

Emphasise and foster intrinsic motivation, not external rewards

This is a vital consideration. Social media encourage all to participate and involve themselves in creative activity because it is intrinsically valuable. There are minimal external rewards associated with involvement. For *Wikipedia*, you may find your name listed somewhere in the history of an article; for *Script Frenzy*, you get a virtual certificate and a Web icon (i.e. not a publishing contract!).

There is a strong message for us as educators. While the extrinsic rewards of doing well in one's education are obvious (e.g. getting good grades in examinations that allow you to progress through the education system), these fade almost into insignificance when compared to the intrinsically motivating and engaging rewards of being involved in the creation and sustaining of *Wikipedia* (over one billion human effort hours and counting). Similarly, the intrinsic motivation that

Script Frenzy empowers for 21,000-plus writers to write over 100 pages is astonishing. New social media challenge us to reconsider, fundamentally, the ways in which we engage (and reward) pupils in their learning.

Recontextualise (do not lose sight of) the individual and their work

This is also crucial. Our education system is rightly concerned with the individual pupil. Whether it be through strategies of differentiation, or approaches to personalisation, it is essential that every pupil is engaged appropriately and challenged through our teaching. However, this focus on making, sharing and connecting for creativity might lead you to think that the social should be prioritised above the individual. This would be wrong. As the *YouTube* example illustrates most clearly, the notion of an individual's work is still important. It has value and should be appreciated at that level.

However, the *YouTube* illustration teaches us that, in one sense, although an individual has finished their work when they upload a video to the site, the journey of that work continues beyond that individual as others take that work, link to it, comment on it, or recontextualise it alongside other pieces of work.

One art teacher explored this process by encouraging her pupils to think about their work in this way. 'Works in progress' (digital photographs of particular pieces of work) were routinely shared on the school intranet. Week by week, she encouraged pupils to spend time giving each other formative feedback. In taking a step back from the role of formal, summative assessment, she empowered her pupils to take a greater degree of responsibility. This had tremendous benefits.

However, this teacher took things one step further. Once digitised, these artworks became source materials for other pupils. Later units of work focused on the issues of sharing, sampling and copyright. She encouraged pupils across the school to liaise with each other through the school intranet, asking them to seek permissions for specific samples of artwork that were then recontextualised in new work. Pupils found this intrinsically motivating and rewarding. At an exhibition of work, done at the end of the school year, many pupils were delighted to see how their ideas had been taken and used in new ways.

What would happen if there was a similar sharing of work on a particular project within your curriculum area? Would it suddenly become more or less important that an individual pupil made a mistake or misunderstood a concept when there was a community of others around who would support and nurture their work in different ways? How would your role, your pedagogy, change within this situation? Would you feel empowered or disempowered? These are fragmentary ideas for us in education, but, increasingly, these are the ways in which young people are used to working. We ignore them at our peril.

Involvement leads to engagement that leads to the potential for change

Perhaps one of the most powerful messages to come out of these illustrations is that an individual's engagement with social media leads to their engagement by social media. It is one thing to discuss these ideas in the abstract. What one really needs to do is engage with them for oneself and appreciate, even feel, the benefits of making, sharing and connecting with others. As we will go on to see in Chapter 6, teachers often feel isolated, both personally and professionally, and find it difficult to make the kinds of social connections of the type we are exploring here within their work. However, Shirky's (2010) model of sharing is intriguing.

Shirky states that personal sharing is simple. Sharing a photograph online is an act of sharing even if no one ever looks at it. There is no additional requirement for the sharer or for the sharee. But that simple process in sharing is the first step in appreciating and engaging with social media. In comparison to personal sharing, creating communal value through sharing is more complicated. It requires participation and interaction on behalf of the group's members to sustain involvement and cohesion. As in the example from the art teacher's work discussed above, there is a higher level of interaction in these types of group through a simple process of personal sharing. There has to be a sense of commitment to a particular cause.

Building a sense of public value relies on and extends this sense of communal value by opening itself up to wider public scrutiny, new ideas and alternatives, and other voices. And in Shirky's fourth level, civic value has the explicit aim of improving the lives of people who never participate within that particular group.

For us as educators, there is a simple application here. We need to instil in our pupils a passion for sharing. Sharing, even in its simplest form, is tied up with making. Making in a fundamental way, as we saw with Gauntlett's ideas early in this chapter, is connecting with others. Sharing, making and connecting are all dimensions of a creative personality.

Summary

Our chapter began with the common idea in education that creativity is an individual attribute. We argued that, while this is pretty much accepted by most writers and theorists, it does not represent the whole truth. Creativity is expressed in various ways. It is often talked of as a process situated within a particular domain and with certain characteristics. We have argued that this is extended and developed in the ways in which people connect together for particular purposes. Our three case studies of an independent computer games developer, a composer and a digital animator gave us an insight into how their creative outputs, that is, what they made, were informed by a whole host of connections and sharing within a particular community.

Drawing on the work of Gauntlett (2011), we rehearsed the idea that making is (and always has been) about connecting. In this sense, creativity is always social. Using stories from Shirky (2008, 2010) and others, we gave examples of these from various social media platforms and then drew some principles from them for our work as educators. There is much more that could be added to this provisional list. We would encourage you to continue thinking through some of the implications of this for your own work. In particular, we would urge you to be an active user of social media for your own personal and professional life. It is only through being an active and willing participant with social media at any level that one can begin to experience its benefits. But while you are doing this, keep an open mind about the educational opportunities and potential that such processes of making, sharing and connecting have for how you teach your own subject. And, while you are doing this, remember that the pupils you teach will, perhaps in a different location or in a different social network, be engaging in similar processes. They will be making, sharing, connecting and engaging in creative processes that will impact on the ways that they think, act and behave within your classroom. Building on these experiences can only help your work as a teacher and facilitate your pupils' learning in powerful ways.

We have drawn on the work of many other writers in support of these claims. One of them, Gauntlett (2011), has summarised most helpfully how the things we deal with in everyday life, creativity and new media come together in five key principles. These are:

- a new understanding of creativity as process, emotion and presence;
- the drive to make and share;
- happiness through creativity and community;
- a middle layer of creativity as social glue;
- making your mark, and making the world your own.

While we have not explored the full impact of these statements within this chapter, the bones of the text have been built around such themes. Gauntlett applies his theory to education specifically, and says:

> This [an anticipated] future education system recognises the characteristics of powerful learners: they are curious about the world, and wish to understand the how and why of things; they have courage, which means they are willing to take risks, and to try things out to see what happens; and they recognise that mistakes are not shameful disasters but are just events that can be learned from. They like to *explore*, *investigate*, and *experiment*. Tinkering with things is a way of learning. They have *imagination*, which is grounded by reason, thoughtfulness, and the ability to plan. They have the virtue of *sociability*, which means they know how to make use of the potent social space of learning. Finally, they are *reflective*, and are aware of their own strengths and weaknesses in the learning process.
>
> (2011: 239)

Gauntlett is a little less clear about the ways in which this transformation will be made possible. In terms of the role of the teacher in all this, he says that pupils will be 'inspired by their teachers, who are no longer just the holders of the "answer book" but are visibly also learning new knowledge and skills in their own lives' (Gauntlett 2011: 237).

We echo these sentiments. But this chapter has advanced a range of other alternatives for you to think about as you seek to build a creative pedagogy inspired by the application of social media. Part of this will be seeking to use the tools themselves. But a much more important element will be seeking to utilise the ways of thinking, the ways of knowing, and the processes of sharing, making and connecting that these tools can bring out. Individual social networks will rise and fall in popularity. But the principles they are built upon have been well theorised, understood and established. We need to build our individual pedagogies having fully appreciated the impact that they play on our own, and our pupils', lives.

In Chapter 6, we are going to continue to examine some of the impact that these new social media platforms have on processes of teaching and learning. In particular, we will explore how they allow users to play, explore, reflect and express themselves in different ways. We will also examine some of the ethical considerations and concerns that they generate.

Discussion points

- While some subjects may seem to be more concerned with making (in a physical sense), how can these concepts be applied to the making/forming of ideas within your own subject area?

- Are there aspects of social media or other networked technologies that militate and work against the creative processes in education?

- How can I begin to open up my pedagogy and share it through new media?

- To what degree am I prepared to allow others to critique what I do as a teacher and allow their approaches to inform my future pedagogy?

Useful websites/resources

http://digitalartsed.ning.com   Digital Arts Education website
www.everythingisaremix.info   *Everything is a Remix* website
www.futurelab.org.uk/resources/connect-why-should-you-use-social-media   *Futurelab* article, 'Connect: why should you use social media?'
www.futurelab.org.uk/resources/curriculum-and-teaching-innovation-handbook   *Futurelab, Curriculum and Teaching Innovation* handbook
www.makingisconnecting.org   David Gauntlett's website, *Making is Connecting*
www.ted.com/index.php/talks/ken_robinson_says_schools_kill_creativity.html   Sir Ken Robinson's talk on schools killing creativity
Sawyer, R. Keith (2007) *Group Genius: The creative power of collaboration*, New York: Basic Books.

References

Arendt, H. (1961) *Between Past and Future: Six exercises in political thought*, London: Faber & Faber.

Boden, M. A. (1990) *The Creative Mind: Myths and mechanisms*, London: Cardinal.

Burgess, J. and Green, J. (2009) 'The entrepreneurial vlogger: participatory culture beyond the professional–amateur divide', in Snickars, P. and Vonerau, P. (eds) *The YouTube Reader*, Stockholm: The National Library of Sweden.

Craft, A. (2000) *Creativity Across the Primary Curriculum: Framing and developing practice*, London: Routledge.

Csikszentmihalyi, M. (1996) *Creativity: Flow and the psychology of discovery and invention*, New York: HarperCollins.

Csikszentmihalyi, M. (1999) 'Implications of a systems perspective for the study of creativity', in Sternberg, R. J. (ed.) *Handbook of Creativity*, Cambridge: Cambridge University Press.

Furedi, F. (2009) *Wasted: Why education isn't educating*, London: Continuum.

Gauntlett, D. (2011) *Making is Connecting: The social meaning of creativity, from DIY and knitting to YouTube and Web 2.0*, Cambridge: Polity.

QCA (Qualifications and Curriculum Authority) (1999) *The National Curriculum: Handbook for secondary teachers in England; Key stages 3 and 4*, London: QCA.

QCDA (Qualifications and Curriculum Development Agency) (2008) *National Curriculum for Key Stage*, London: QCDA. Available online: http://curriculum.qcda.gov.uk (accessed 15 March 2011).

Script Frenzy (2011) 'Couldn't someone just write the same sentence for 100 pages and say they won?' Available online: www.scriptfrenzy.org/eng/node/120304 (accessed 9 May 2011).

Shirky, C. (2008) *Here Comes Everybody*, New York: Allen Lane.

Shirky, C. (2010) *Cognitive Surplus: Creativity and generosity in a connected age*, New York/London: Penguin Press.

Wallas, G. (1926) *The Art of Thought*, New York: Harcourt, Brace.

6

The impact of digital networked technologies on teaching and learning

Key questions

■ How can key human processes such as playing, exploring, reflecting and expressing be developed through the use of digital networked technologies?

■ What ethical issues do I need to consider as I use these new technologies within the classroom?

Playing, exploring, reflecting, and expressing are behaviours that are central to human experience. Education has always harnessed them for the purposes of teaching and learning, and technology has always, in many ways, been developed to augment them. So, in this chapter we will look at how online games and virtual worlds have been used to enhance play; how social bookmarking, tagging and recommending systems enhance our explorations; how blogs, social networks and wikis add to our capacity to reflect; and how media-sharing, manipulation and remixing are enabling us to express ourselves in new and very creative ways. As we do so, we will examine the impacts of these new enhancing tools for education. Finally, we will show how these technologies can be glued together to constitute a dynamic learning environment for use within your own teaching.

Technologies are not value-free. They raise ethical questions that we need to engage with. Ever since the advent of the Internet and the World Wide Web, concerns have been expressed about issues such as online predators, illegal downloading, inappropriate posting of private materials to public forums and online bullying. In response, a number of cyber-safety initiatives have developed in the UK to keep children and young people safe on the Internet. Many of these have been coordinated by the UK Council for Child Internet Safety (UKCCIS).[1] UKCCIS, established in 2008, coordinates both research into internet safety[2] and educational campaigns for parents and children,[3] as well as resources for schools such as the extensive and very good collection at ThinkUKnow (TUK), the teachers' and trainers' section of the Child Exploitation and Online Protection Area,[4] and those provided by Childnet International.[5]

As you begin to develop ways of introducing digital media technologies into your classrooms or extend their use in ways we suggest in this chapter, these resources constitute essential reading.

Our intention is not to repeat or attempt a summary of them here. Instead, as we discuss emerging technologies and their use in education, we will introduce ethical issues and questions for you to think through. We will do that around four areas that we think are under an ethical spotlight as digital networked technologies become ubiquitous: identity, trust, privacy and ownership. For ease of presentation, an ethical area is presented for each emerging set of technologies. However, ethical issues are not easily 'boxed up' into discrete areas. Issues of identity, which we explore in the section on social play, are equally important in online social networks where we focus on issues of privacy, and vice versa. Bear this in mind as you read through the chapter.

Reflective task

Before you read ahead, what types of ethical questions or issues could you imagine might arise from the use of the technologies we are going to discuss in this chapter? Can you think of any practical examples of these issues that have arisen in your teaching to this point?

Playing: online games and virtual worlds

Case study 6.1

The simulation begins with the creation of two fundamentally different groups, Alpha and Beta. The Alpha group is a 'high-context' patriarchal culture where relationships, physical closeness and cooperation are highly prized values. Greetings take the form of formulaic rituals. There is a great deal of phatic communication, and physical touch is encouraged. Beta, on the other hand, is a culture where who you are is based on what you trade. It is competitive and meritocratic. For the Beta group, 'Time is money'. Language is shaped by trading and values are negotiated in a non-hierarchical way.

In preparation for the simulation the two groups, in separate spaces, practise the cultural behaviour and language conventions of their group until they feel confident and can act fluently within the rules they have been given. The actual simulation involves the exchange of visitors from each culture. One member of the Alpha culture visits the Beta culture (and vice versa), interacts and returns 'home' to share their experiences. The initial reactions tend to revolve around feelings of alienation, isolation and confusion as, one after another, members of one culture begin to adapt to a new culture and its ways of interacting.

More visitors are exchanged. Hunches about the new culture are experimented with in situ with often frustrating results. Members of each culture are actively trying to understand the other, interact successfully with the other and solve similar problems to the other. But it is difficult. After the exchanges are complete, the simulation ends and debriefing begins by probing the participants: What did you think of Alphans/Betans? How did Alphans/Betans behave when in your culture? How did that make you feel? How did it feel to be in another culture? How did you cope when 'rejected' by that culture? How did the rules for appropriate behaviour emerge? What were the rules? What have you learned? Are there ways in which what you have learned can be applied in your lives or work?

Using online games in education

This simulation, *Bafa' Bafa'*,[6] is a very well-known activity that has been used throughout the world since the 1970s by educators, corporate managers and trainers, healthcare workers and government employees to explore cultural differences and their impact at a personal and organisational level. The value of the activity is that it is experiential. Participants are made personally aware of culture differences through the feelings of alienation and confusion that come from being different. They also experience the power of shared knowledge and emerging understanding as, together, they begin to make sense of the 'other'. Finally, as one group, they are able to rethink their behaviour and focus on how they perceive and understand difference.

Bafa' Bafa' is a role-play simulation game. It is a 'microworld' that models, somewhat simplistically, a real-world environment in order to help participants develop an understanding of, and competence in, working with culturally diverse groups. As a learning task the game exploits our propensity to learn by mimicking, playing and experimenting: following up hunches with practical action and reflecting on that action to move forward.

Bafa' Bafa' seldom provokes educational controversy. We have used it many times with diverse groups in different contexts. Rarely have we had to explain that it is a serious game with outcomes that transcend the fun that participants may have in playing it.

However, once we begin to talk about online games, gaming and education, there is a sense that we are entering into a debate that is inherently controversial. Perhaps it is the terminology. 'Game' does evoke the idea in many of a card or board game or simply of an activity that is restricted to children. Perhaps it is the negative press given to games in much of mainstream media (with headlines such as: 'I was a games addict';[7] 'Computer games make pupils too tired to learn';[8] 'Teeth take a hit when computer games lead to bad bites'[9]), the lack of experience that many teachers have with the intensely complex, immersive virtual worlds that constitute such games as *World of Warcraft*[10] and *Club Penguin*,[11] or the pressures of a curriculum and assessment system that sees such games as exclusively after-school activities.

Yet there is little doubt about the importance and popularity of the medium. Both *World of Warcraft* and *Club Penguin*, among the most popular of the massively multiplayer online role-playing games (MMORPGs) claim to have over 12 million active subscribers – more than the population of Greece. The virtual world research firm, *KZero*, reported over one billion registered accounts across all virtual worlds in 2011, a number dominated by those in the 10–15 age group.[12]

These games take place in online 'virtual worlds' – screen environments that allow users to navigate around the space and interact with others through avatars. While gaming can be a solitary or single-player activity, in these environments it is a highly collaborative one. In MMORPGs players often work in virtual teams on specific tasks and challenges that demand effective communication and literacy skills. Research has begun to explore such skills and their value for schools (Becta 2006; Williamson 2009; Wastiau et al. 2009). Steinkuehler's two-year ethnographic study into literacy practices in MMORPGs explored how reading and writing practices consisted of making sense, producing meaning and making decisions from an enormous array of multimedia resources. She describes how such meaning-making involves reading and writing large amounts of text in genres as wide-ranging as letter-writing, poetry, narrative and instructions. She concludes that such practices mirror those that are most valued in the education system and argues that there is great potential to use online games for learning. In thinking of games as learning environments, Steinkuehler suggests: 'we can discern design principles in games that might fruitfully be applied to the design of educational technologies, be they classrooms, after-school clubs, or corporate training retreats' (2008: 18).

Those design principles are now becoming much easier to employ in the development of games. Thanks to game engines, games middleware and mods (modified versions of existing games), it is now possible for people with little or no programming knowledge to develop digital games. This means that teachers can now create games that focus on particular curriculum areas or skills. *Game Maker*,[13] a free and simple game engine, allows teachers to develop their own games, find support from a community in doing so and test out their creations before using them in a school context.

Perhaps the most well-known virtual world, *Second Life*[14] brings together thousands of users daily who design avatars, build communities and interact with and in their environments. While *Second Life* does not have game-like rules, it does allow development and experimentation in simulations and (role) play. Teachers have used *Second Life* to simulate medical environments, immerse history students in virtual ancient cities, involve architecture students in modelling specific buildings with detailed 'footfalls', and (with the use of Linden dollars, the *Second Life* currency) run prototype retail initiatives.

Julie Sykes, a doctoral student at the University of Minnesota, designed a virtual world, *Croquelandia*, in order to explore the value of immersive worlds for language learning and the development of authentic intercultural communication skills. *Croquelandia* is described as an environment where participants, through adopted simulated identities, can practise language in diverse social settings; where meaningful language use can be practised in a low-risk environment; and where an emotional connection to the language can be forged through the ethnographic experience of 'being there' (Sykes et al. 2008).

In a sense, we have come full circle. If *Bafa' Bafa'* became an uncontroversial role-play simulation through being experientially effective – it is a good game – the kinds of games that are emerging from our understandings of MMORPGs may well achieve the same. They may become more integrated into schools as game-like forms of learning. James Paul Gee expressed such a view in an interview with Henry Jenkins: 'Deep learning is achieved when learners are focused on well designed, well ordered, and well mentored problem solving with shared goals, that is, goals shared with mentors and a learning community' (Jenkins 2011).

Ethical reflection: identity play

When we turn to the ethics of online games and virtual worlds, there are a number of issues that we need to examine. We need to understand how game play expresses ethical behaviour and how ethical behaviour is built into game-like learning. We also need to investigate the relationship between game-worlds online and life offline beyond the public relations hype that online games are 'good' for you, or the moral panics generated in the media. Above all, we need to begin to engage with the ethical frameworks that games are presenting to young people in order to appreciate when, where and how they might be used to promote the kind of 'deep learning' that James Paul Gee argues is possible.

Online games revolve around actions, interactions and choices. What, then, are the actions and choices that are available to game players in a particular game? Decisions about such actions and choices are made at a variety of levels.

Game developers make choices about who can do what, when and with whom. These actions are coded into the game itself. What kind of violence is acceptable in a first-person shooter game such as *Medal of Honor*? Is simulated killing coded into the pleasure of playing? What components are available for the construction of avatars in *World of Warcraft*? What relationships can such avatars engage in? How do demographics affect the decisions that are made about such coding?

Publishers of online games similarly make choices about how the controversy around particular games might attract users and increase profits. They make decisions about the nature of their responsibility not only to the online gaming community, but also to wider society in ways that might set precedents for legislation.

Marketers make decisions about how to attract users, how to sell subscriptions and how to increase the user-base. In particular, their work is concerned with positioning children and young people (and their parents) within markets in order, largely, to 'monetise' their presence online.

Finally, game players themselves make choices about the games they play, the rules they follow, the rules they are prepared to break and what they are prepared to do to 'win', as well as the role that online games play in their lives. We need to engage critically with these issues and we need to design ways of increasing young people's critical engagement with them. But, you might be thinking, does this matter? It is, after all, 'just a game'.

One answer to this question suggests that games are like walled gardens. This is a view most often attributed to Johan Huizinga, who thought of games as central to what it means to be human. He argued that games were protected by a 'magic circle', or bounded space, which sets them apart from the everyday (Huizinga 1955). If you take this view you might argue that, while it would be wrong, and you would be prosecuted for leaving a real pet tied up in a real shed without real food or water until it really died, it would be inappropriate to judge the same behaviour in the same way if it took place in *Incrediland*[15] (where you can raise virtual pets from eggs to adults). The advantage of this view is that it frees us from the ethical demands of real life in order to explore a wide variety of ethical actions and their consequences. Online game players can make big mistakes without suffering big consequences. Players can try out what it means to act in ways that are 'wrong'. Fantasy is freed from ethical constraints.

But how strong are the 'boundaries' of the magic circle? Is the wall impervious? MMORPGs and virtual worlds ask that you construct, edit and perform a self through an avatar. Once we begin to design an avatar to play *World of Warcraft* or join *Second Life* we begin to make choices: what name to adopt; what to look like; what clothes to wear. The possibilities are endless, yet they are all informed by our hopes, strengths and weaknesses. Our online identity is informed by us. The walled garden begins to seem rather more porous.

As educators, many of our practices have been designed in ways that provide supportive environments where the guided explorations and healthy play of such work can take place. With so many young people now doing that work online, in virtual worlds, we need to use that experience, together with a greater understanding of the virtual worlds they inhabit, to better support their development.

Practical task

Given that many young people play games online regularly, it is an important part of your own professional development to be aware of these environments and the challenges, opportunities or threats that they contain. While you might not think of yourself as a 'gamer', why not spend some time exploring one of the games mentioned above? As you play, think through some of the ethical questions and issues raised. The following questions can help you get started on this:

- How strong are the boundaries in this game? Is the game like a 'walled garden' or are the boundaries more porous? Does the virtual world' relate to the 'physical' in any meaningful ways?

- How are different identities constructed within the game? Who decides what is possible, achievable or desirable?

- What choices can I make within the game environment? How are these regulated (if at all)?

- Finally, having explored the game environment, what potential does it hold for the processes of teaching and learning within your subject area? Are there developments in this area that you can pursue further, perhaps through resources such as *Game Maker*?

Exploring: bookmarking, tagging and recommending

In Chapter 2 we discussed the acceleration of information available and how we could reduce the possible cognitive and creative paralysis that this might induce by reframing our understanding of information as social. Thinking of the Web as the social networking of people and information allows us to think that our own contributions to the conversation are not only possible but actually necessary. What the suggestion does not provide an answer to is the following question: how do we navigate these various (social) information flows?

Imagine that you are looking for a particular product, say a new gate for your garden. Searching online reveals hundreds of options, all the right size but with contrasting styles and prices. You narrow down your options, but even then you have countless potential suppliers to choose from and numerous prices, some including postage and packing, others offering various additional components designed to make installing your gate 'easier'. Swamped with information, we might throw up our hands and return to the tried and trusted Yellow Pages, phone up a local fencing company and rely on the expertise of a particular tradesperson.

While planning a lesson, we start searching for something online. Hours later we find ourselves reading a web page that we had no intention of reading. We have followed links that have taken us far, far away from our initial search query. At that point, we might return to the calm of the library where the routines and rituals of information retrieval are tried and trusted; we find what we were looking for.

If you recognise the two scenarios above you are likely to be a teacher rather than a student – someone who knows their way around the local bookshops as they do the school library. The reason we know our way around these collections is that they have been organised: crime fiction upstairs, reference collections on the ground floor. Such information, information about information, is known as metadata.

Libraries have used this kind of metadata and held it in card catalogues for hundreds of years to make access to a library's collection easier. The best known of these systems is the Dewey Decimal Classification system introduced by Melvil Dewey in the United States in 1876. Dewey created a hierarchical list of all topics of knowledge, starting with philosophy then religion followed by the social sciences, language, natural sciences, mathematics, technology, arts and recreation, literature and rhetoric, and ending up with geography, history and biography.

The rigidness of Dewey's system is also, however, its great weakness: one book cannot be in two places at the same time. If I am interested in *Google* and its various applications and I browse the educational technology section, I will not find *The University of Google*. However, if that book is in digital form then it can be in different places at the same time at no increased cost. In fact it can be in any 'place' that users of the book might find it useful to be. It could be in a virtual pile of information labelled 'review essay'; it could be in a collection labelled 'cyber-pessimists'; in another labelled '*Google*'; or another 'teaching'. It could be in all of those collections at the same time. This is what is meant by the term 'folksonomy' (a blend of 'folk' and 'taxonomy'), coined by Thomas Vander Wal in 2005 to refer to the practice of collaborative categorisation of information using keywords or 'tags' (Peters 2009: 154). It is a bottom-up organising principle in which there are no experts and a system that is, at best, 'emergent'.

When we discussed *Twitter* in Chapter 3 (see page 50), we referred to the practice of following hashtags such as #ukedchat. We can filter the results of a search of *Twitter* by using #ukedchat, which will retrieve all those tweets that share the same hashtag. Instead of authoritative categories and terminology, users of documents or other pieces of information create a link to a resource through a 'bookmark' and then assign categories, labels or specialised terminology to indicate what the resource is. They have created a shorthand system for finding information. The tagger can change, delete and link tags. Tags can be used by one person to organise their resources, much like the 'favourites' feature in web browsers.

However, tags are also intended to express a user's understanding of particular resources to others and this makes them inherently social. Services such as *delicious*,[16] *diigo*[17] and *furl*[18] aggregate tags across the Web, making the folksonomies broader and very different from the top-down standardised, taxonomic classification schemes such as the Dewey system. In place of the hierarchical systems of nested lists described above, folksonomies are better represented by the 'tag clouds' that have become a familiar feature of social network sites.

Services that aggregate tags also aggregate 'user + tag', allowing networks to be created between users on the basis of their understandings of particular resources through their tagging behaviour. Using, for example, the tag 'social-bookmarking' on a number of resources not only allows me to collect and

Figure 6.1 Screen shot of author's *delicious* tag cloud

retrieve those resources, but *delicious* also allows me to see those resources that have been tagged 'socialbookmarking' by all users of *delicious*, as well as filtering those results to include only those users who are in my network. Using multiple tags and Boolean operators allows resources to be further refined. This system of aggregating tags and users makes it possible to build collaborative repositories of related information driven by personal interest and creative organisation.

We should not underestimate the role of *Google* in the expansion of folksonomic tagging. *Google* is an example of a 'natural language' search tool that allows users to search for resources using whatever search terms seem most appropriate to them. *Google*'s search results, based on their proprietary Page Rank algorithm, are highly relevant, given the enormous levels of data and analytical tools that are used to create them. However, as librarians often argue, *Google*'s bias towards 'natural language' often precludes the use of terms that are very specific to particular fields or disciplines. We are unlikely to consult a thesaurus of technical terms before searching with *Google*. What we are more likely to do, however, and what we now have the tools to do, is to be our own librarians, collecting and curating our resources, exploring and discovering for ourselves and for others. The strength of natural language searching and folksonomies is that they can be personalised, adapted and used creatively. They open all kinds of possibilities.

Practical task

If you have not done so already, create an account with a social bookmarking service such as *delicious*. Identify a unit of work that you are going to be teaching to a class in the near future (e.g. a unit of work on the poetry of Seamus Heaney). Compile a list of resources for use within the unit (e.g. recordings of Heaney reciting his poems, historical information about his life and work, other interpretations of his poems, his influences, etc.). Create a social bookmark for each one. As you explore, use the recommender system to help find alternative resources to your own sources. These might take your thinking and planning for the unit of work in new directions.

As you start to teach the unit, share your social bookmarks with your pupils. Give them the opportunity to begin to extend the collection of resources through their own tagging of other materials and resources that they find online.

Consider the following questions:

■ What advantages or disadvantages have there been to your use of this tool?

- Has it affected your planning, your teaching or your pupils' learning in new ways?

- As pupils become familiar with this process, how might it affect the ways in which you might teach future units?

- Is the process of following others' links, recommendations or resources conducive to the processes of learning that you are trying to facilitate within your classroom?

Ethical reflection: when is a crowd a mob?

For several years, Web 2.0 technologies have been harnessing the participatory, social sharing of information to build insights from users of those technologies. The idea that the collective opinion of a group of individuals can be more valid and valuable than the ideas of a single expert has gained currency as new ways of aggregating individuals' use of the Web are emerging. The idea is the same as that used in the popular television game show, *Who Wants to Be a Millionaire?*, when the contestant, unsure of an answer, asks the audience. The collective knowledge of the group is more likely to produce the correct answer than the knowledge of one individual. The book *The Wisdom of Crowds: Why the many are smarter than the few and how collective wisdom shapes business, economies, societies and nations* (Surowiecki 2005) deftly summarises the main idea in its title.

In the world of Web 2.0 it has been the idea of bottom-up collaboration and user participation that has begun to solve the problem of information retrieval. Through tagging, rating, reviewing and recommending we have made it easier for ourselves to retrieve information in a more targeted way, rather than the aimless clicking through pages of search results. Websites now consistently use such user input to influence what information is given priority to whom. However, there is a problem with this system. If only half of the audience in *Who Wants to Be a Millionaire?* offer an answer, the collective intelligence of the whole group is skewed. In other words, crowd-sourcing solutions demand the active participation of members of the crowd. Not everyone is motivated to participate and even those who are do so for different reasons. Those who contribute to *Rate My Professors*[19] may be motivated by the need to rant about a negative experience with a teacher rather than by an altruistic desire to help others. In either case, we can never know.

The negative implications of this have been explored most notably by Andrew Keen in *The Cult of the Amateur: How today's Internet is killing our culture and assaulting our economy* (2007). He argues that, rather than inaugurating an epoch of collective intelligence, user participation is destroying the role of the expert and making it more and more difficult to find quality and trustworthy information online. When the crowd is hailed as the great leveller, the expert loses authority and knowledge and culture suffer. If everyone is considered an authority, who can be trusted? The professional journalist is threatened by the collective expression of amateur bloggers. The teacher is challenged by the collective activity of ratings and reviews. Keen is worried that, with the loss of faith in authority, we are creating a collection of opinions instead of truth. That partial collection represents those who shout the loudest through their Web 2.0 tools. That particular majority creates a pressure to homogenise based on principles that are increasingly remote from real people. When presented with 'recommendations' to tag a particular piece of information in a particular way – to 'like' on the basis of other people's 'likes' – we follow the crowd. Clearly, there are consequences. With characteristic pessimism, Keen thinks of it as the blind leading the blind: where 'ignorance meets egoism meets bad taste meets mob rule' (ibid.: 1). One of the consequences of that is that mob rule marginalises, hurts and offends.

Keen offers an alternative view to those who argue that collective intelligence and crowd-sourcing are only a force for good. He reminds us that perhaps the crowds are not so wise after all. In doing so he challenges us to think of the consequences of the anarchic tagging and sharing of information. If we are uneasy with those consequences, we need to think of ways in which 'moderation' should take place and by whom. We also need to think about how to create mechanisms that we can trust to connect content to people with credentials we can trust. The ethical challenge in our own online (and offline) activity is to cultivate genuine credibility by being truthful, transparent and taking responsibility about what we do and why we do it. As Douglas Rushkoff comments:

> The less we take responsibility for what we say and do online, the more likely we are to behave in ways that reflect our worst natures – or even the worst natures of others. Because digital technology is biased toward depersonalisation, we must make every effort not to operate anonymously, unless absolutely necessary. We must be ourselves.
>
> (2011: 83)

Practical task

In Chapter 3 we talked about the ways in which we participate in the *Twitter*-based public discussion #ukedchat (see page 53). For this task we would like you to browse the archives of these public discussions. Summaries of these are available on the ukedchat blog (http://ukedchat.wordpress.com) and full discussions are archived on the ukedchat wiki (http://ukedchat.wikispaces.com). You do not need a *Twitter* account to complete the task.

As you read through these discussions make a note of the mechanisms that are used to ensure that a community of trust is built and maintained. Because this is a *Twitter* discussion group the contributors all have *Twitter* names (@deerwood is an example). Copy and paste two or three of these names into a search engine.

- What do you learn about these contributors?
- Does what you learn increase the credibility of their contributions?
- What role does the moderator play in the discussions?

While the archives give you an understanding of the nature of online public discussions, the best way of assessing their use is to actively participate. Join #ukedchat, contribute to the discussions, reflect on your learning and the nature of the particular channel. If the experience is positive, you might also think how it could be replicated with your own pupils.

Reflecting: blogs and social networks

Blogs are web-based journals or, more simply, personal websites. Short for 'web logs', blogs provide a range of communication and publishing functions for specific interests such as canoe-building to broad categories such as politics and science. It is difficult to calculate how many blogs there are online. The blogging search engine *Technorati*[20] has indexed over 133 million since 2002, but many may have been started and abandoned and some may be very irregularly updated. Our own first experiences of posting to a blog had a revolutionary excitement to it. There was nobody to ask for permission to 'publish', no editor and no 'publication'. And at that click of the mouse we really did think 'now any reader on the net can read that!' Of course, over time we have become a little more sanguine about our possible reach and recognise that our current blogs garner a relatively limited readership.

We have also begun to recognise that being an 'author' is only part of the reason why the activity of blogging is revolutionary. In an article in *The Atlantic*, the journalist Andrew Sullivan makes the point elegantly. The blogger, he says:

> is – more than any writer of the past – a node among other nodes, connected but unfinished without the links and the comments and the track-backs that make the blogosphere, at its best, a conversation, rather than a production.
>
> (2008)

It is the conversation that makes blogging a collective, social enterprise and not just an individual act of authorship. Conversation starts with the links we provide to the sources we cite as our thoughts develop and arguments build. We share and manage information on our blogs. The links we make to other resources on the Web evidence our claims and those links between blogs, between articles, to and from various websites, drive more people to read our posts. As Sullivan says:

> One of the most prized statistics in the blogosphere is therefore not the total number of readers or page views, but the 'authority' you get by being linked to by other blogs. It's an indication of how central you are to the online conversation of humankind.
>
> (ibid.)

Blogging shows just how interactive our new publishing paradigm is: a dynamic, always unfinished conversation.

There has been a flourishing education blogosphere for a number of years where teachers and academics maintain personal or professional blogs as well as using blogs in various ways in teaching, particularly as a tool for encouraging and teaching writing. Recent research by the National Literacy Trust suggests that such use is valuable. Their 2009 survey of 3,001 children aged between 9 and 16 found that 24 per cent had their own blog and that 'young people who write on a blog were more likely than young people who do not write on a blog to enjoy writing in general and to enjoy writing for family/friends in particular' (Clark and Dugdale 2009: 34). They claim no causal link in these findings – children may blog because they write well or blogging may be a way of improving writing – yet the survey does suggest that fears over the adoption of such 'open' tools seem to be unfounded and that such tools do drive enthusiasm for writing.

One of the largest educational blogging communities on the Web is *Edublogs*,[21] which offers free hosting for a Wordpress-powered blog, advice on using blogs with pupils in school and how to start conversations using the blog. They currently host over 400,000 blogs. Every year *Edublogs* coordinates a Student Blog Challenge over a ten-week period, designed to improve students' blogging and commenting skills and encourage links between a global network of school-based bloggers.[22] In 2010, over 700 blogs from more than ten countries were involved in the challenge. *Radio Waves*, a UK social learning site, began in 2003 and now has more than 1,300 schools using its services, uploading blog posts, podcasts and videos and sharing within a 'registered users only' international community.[23]

The Education Blog Awards celebrate blogging in UK schools. In 2011, Ferry Lane Primary School in London entered the competition for the 'Class Blog of the Year'. Jack Sloan, a teacher at the school, explains what impact blogging has had on two of his Year 5 pupils, Jozef and Sharon. Jozef arrived at the school from Slovakia in 2010. Every week the class publishes a post on 'Free stuff to do in London this weekend'.

> Each week Jozef tells the class where he has been. He is being exposed to language and experiences that are helping him and his family to learn

English rapidly. He has taken part in painting classes at Somerset House, been bird-watching at nearby Tottenham Marshes, been to the macabre 'Cryptmas' fair, and visited some of our country's best museums. These experiences are vital for rich language acquisition, and something that I feel we need to promote heavily in our school. Through the 'Free stuff to do' blog posts, Jozef is learning about the world around him and this is, I feel, having a significant impact on his education. He is becoming more articulate and more engaged with his learning, and is sharing some rich experiences with his family.[24]

Sharon expresses her own experience with the power and potential of publishing through a blog. Here she explains why the class blogs:

A blog is a website where you learn how to improve your writing and to play games ... BLAAH, BLAAH! Oh come on, think outside of the box. Of course you will learn to improve your work. However, when have you ever thought that billions of people from around the whole world would even bother to comment on your work? Well it has happened, and you'll never guess who commented on my work. No it wasn't an Arsenal football player, or Cheryl Cole. In fact it was someone ten times better. VALERIE BLOOM!! You know, the famous poet, an inspiration to all. I just came to school like regular and all I heard for the rest of the day was 'Oh Sharon you lucky girl, Valerie Bloom commented on your work AAH!' I felt like fainting (literally!) And from that day forth I had a term full of opportunities glimmering in your heart.[25]

Social networks allow users to create digital identities (profiles) for themselves, allow 'friends' to access their online space, cultivate relationships by posting updates, commenting on others' spaces and sharing digital materials (photographs, videos), and join groups that share common interests. Over the past five years social network sites have become the most prominent sites on the Web. The more well-known sites such as *MySpace*,[26] *Bebo*[27] and *Facebook* have now been joined by more specialist social network sites such as *LinkedIn*[28] (focusing on business and professional connections), *Multiply*[29] (social networking plus shopping) and those enabling users to create their own (*Ning*[30]). Sites such as *YouTube* and *Flickr* also have social network capabilities built into them, allowing communities to develop around specific shared interests.

The use of *Facebook* in the last five years has exploded with more than 600 million registered users worldwide in 2011. In the UK, research by the London School of Economics for the European Commission shows that 43 per cent of 9–12-year-olds and 88 per cent of 13–16-year-olds maintain a social network profile (Livingstone et al. 2011). Such ubiquity has led many to look to harness the collaborative and cooperative qualities of social network sites in formal educational settings. Our pupils and students are already using social networks informally to get support from their peers in school-related tasks and to discuss homework and teachers, as well as checking timetables and coordinating their academic activities.

The argument is that, by supporting interaction between learners, encouraging the development of peer-based shared understandings and enabling mutual support and discussion spaces (Maloney 2007), social network sites can be valuable platforms in formal education. While some teachers welcome the opportunity for positive social networking with students (Lemuel 2006; Mazer et al. 2007), many are reluctant to 'import' *Facebook* into schools. Some are trying innovative solutions by using the platform to build secure applications that encourage content creation, sharing and play (Greenhow 2011). Others worry about issues of privacy and the vulnerabilities of children and of a profession under '*Facebook* scrutiny'. Perhaps the most visible uses of social network sites, however, in educational contexts are those that are dedicated to professional development. Sites such as *Learn Central*,[31] *Classroom 2.0*,[32] *Edubuzz*[33] and the *School of Everything*,[34] offer support for peer learning and exploration by and for teachers.

The educational importance of social networks appears to be their use in informal contexts outside school. Using social networks to bridge the gap between informal learning at home and formal school learning is only beginning to be explored. As it is, a number of questions are emerging around issues such as safety and privacy on social networks, which are driving schools towards 'dealing with' social network sites. In some cases, 'dealing with' involves teaching the kinds of literacies that are needed to engage effectively with such sites. In others, it involves a refusal to engage with them at all.

For some schools mobile phone technology has no place in the classroom. Others are thinking differently. One head teacher we talked to insisted that all the children bring their mobiles to school and leave them on unless told otherwise during class time. The school registered each phone on a central system and so was able easily to communicate anything important, such as a change of class or a change of venue. Class teachers also used the system to 'nudge' pupils to complete their homework. Pupils themselves were able to communicate easily with the school if they needed to. Because the pupils tend to Bluetooth each other when they are in school, the school could also track attendance. This 'solution' to the ubiquity of mobile phones would have appeared at best unfeasible and at worst 'Orwellian' five years ago. The kinds of issues that are currently being debated with regard to social networking in schools just might follow the same trajectory. More and more teachers are using social networks for learning. They are blogging, creating vlogs and listening to podcasts. They are attending online conferences where communities are built up and become resources for future learning. They are also writing texts using wikis, sharing their ideas in tweets and re-tweets and following conversations about pedagogy, curriculum development and teaching tools. The enthusiasm of this grass-roots activity is infectious and it will infect the solutions to the issues around the educational use of digital social networking in schools and out of them. Those solutions are likely to be increasingly creative.

Reflective task

The extensive use of social networking software such as *Facebook* can create problematic questions that go to the heart of what we consider a teacher should be and how they should behave. How would you respond to the following questions:

- As a teacher, should you be on *Facebook* at all?

- Should you be worried about what you publish on *Facebook* or any other social sharing space on the Web?

- Should you accept a 'friend' request from a current student on your personal profile?

- Should you limit your use of *Facebook* to a personal network and not use it as a place where learning should be discussed?

Ethical reflection: privacy, does it matter?

There are very few people who do not have something on the Internet that they would rather people not see. Examples from our past include embarrassing photos, discussion post rants, blog posts and comments that we have regretted writing. As young people document their lives more and more assiduously on the Web, and as search technology for obtaining information on people on the Internet improves, the possibility of forgetting those moments is becoming increasingly difficult. Our digital footprint might recede into the distant past, but it is never likely to be completely invisible. Rather than footprints, our digital records are beginning to look more like tattoos. Privacy is an issue.

Recent research suggests that teenagers are concerned about privacy and aspire towards achieving greater privacy in their online activities. In fact, more young adults actively control their privacy settings in social network sites than do older people (Hoofnagle et al. 2010). We have to harness this concern and move it beyond the tweaking of privacy settings (though these are vital) towards a more careful management of the boundaries through which privacy is actually expressed, as well as a more critical understanding of the organisations that facilitate the social sharing of information.

The management of boundaries was much easier in an exclusively offline world. Teaching colleagues and staffroom friends, neighbours, tennis partners and old school friends tended to coexist in separate silos and, unless you had one of those parties where you tried to mix them together (with often disastrous results), rarely did one group come into contact with another. However, the online networks that we are creating do not generally match those offline networks. There is no way of representing, online, the nuanced offline friendship groups. There are only 'friends' on *Facebook* – special friends are not allowed. So the 'updates' that I am able to selectively manage between my various offline groups have no equivalents online. All my friends are updated with all my news. This can have unintended consequences when sharing, for example, a photograph intended for one 'audience' with another for whom it was not intended.

Two factors complicate this story. The first is that the feature driving the success of social network sites such as *Facebook* is that the more personal information you reveal, the larger, and potentially more useful, your social network is likely to be. This is true of many Web 2.0 sites. We are encouraged to share our personal information in order to benefit from the (social) network effect. We 'over-share' in order to gain the kind of attention that will generate even larger social networks.

The second factor concerns the portability of a social network. Many websites now allow *Facebook Connect* to enable new visitors to use their *Facebook* usernames and passwords to register an account with them. That option results in both the *Facebook* profile and the social network of connections moving to the new account. Many *Facebook* applications take advantage of the same idea. Social networks (social graphs in the language of *Facebook*) are expanded into different services with enormous ease. The connections increase but the social network as described in terms of 'connected friends' has not become more nuanced.

As the Web becomes more social and personal, the need to manage the flows of information becomes more urgent. There is a real danger of losing control. Disclosing personal information, together with the tendency to over-share, is built into the technology. One ethical challenge therefore, is to care enough about privacy to be proactive in protecting it. The default setting in the Social Web is 'public'. But the 'public' is becoming a fuzzy concept. As danah boyd puts it: 'What's at stake here is often not about whether or not something is public or private, but how public or private it is' (boyd, 2010). We need to claim the private when the private is what we expect, as well as manage the public when the public is what we intend. This is especially true in public identities as visible as that of 'The Teacher', where boyd worries about:

> How public is she allowed to be online? Is she allowed to be religious or secular depending on your community? Can she have an online dating profile? Can she post pictures of her drinking with her friends on a public website? Is she allowed to be a lover and a friend in a public setting where she's always The Teacher? Offline, she knows how to switch into being Teacher when she runs into you and your child on the streets; how does she do that switch online?
>
> (ibid.)

There are no simple answers – no formula that will cover all eventualities. Instead, as we try to answer such questions for ourselves, we should take the opportunity to engage the young people we teach with the same questions.

Expressing: media sharing, manipulation and remixing

In 1999, Shawn Manning established a central index of the music his friends had stored on their computers so that they could all share their favourite songs over the Internet. After some experimentation, coding, and the purchase of a web server and website, *Napster* was born. Very soon, 25 million people were downloading tracks from each other using Manning's central server. It was clearly illegal and within two years a court order forced it to close due to copyright infringement.

However, the idea of peer-to-peer sharing was incubated and, when the central server that acted as an exchange linking the users together was removed, the concept remained. As a result, a new generation of so-called file-sharing systems emerged that eliminated the need of a central server. Systems such as *Kazaa*,[35] *LimeWire*[36] and *BitTorrent*[37] were launched and, although they have continued to come under pressure through copyright laws, they are much harder to prosecute. The level of file-sharing through such systems has grown enormously. It is now estimated that between 44 and 79 per cent of global internet traffic is dedicated to file-sharing (ipoque 2006).

While the practice of users sharing music through peer-to-peer networks has largely been based on copying commercial materials, a number of services have emerged for the legal sharing of music (*Jamendo*[38] and *Spotify*[39]) that use free-to-share Creative Commons licensing, involve a subscription charge or include aural advertising. There are also very recognisable silos for the sharing of user-generated content, including photo-sharing (through sites such as *Flickr*[40]), artwork (*Deviant Art*[41]), slideshow presentations (*Slideshare*[42]), lectures and conference presentations (*Academic Earth*,[43] *VideoLectures*[44]), and video sharing (*YouTube*,[45] *Vimeo*[46]). These last, in particular, tend to be a mixture of reused film or TV materials and home-made video clips. Combined with the practice of social bookmarking, peer rating and the inclusion of comments, the power of sharing digital media is increasing exponentially. It can surprise even the most conservative media observer.

In 2007, Michael Wesch, a cultural anthropologist at Kansas State University in the US, uploaded a four-and-a-half-minute video to *YouTube* and called it *Web 2.0 … The Machine is Us/ing Us*.[47] The video examines the power of digital text and the ways it is restructuring how we think about information and the world. It is at once simple and complex. Captivating editing techniques, plus a catchy soundtrack, present a series of Web 2.0 possibilities. Within five days of uploading the video it had been watched over 30,000 times and, by the end of the sixth day, 91,000 times (Powers, 2007). At the time of writing, the video has been viewed over 11 million times.

To make the video, Wesch used *Camstudio*, a free screen recorder, an open-source editing suite to edit the video, and part of a song from an Ivory Coast musician named Deus who released his track through a Creative Commons licence on *Jamendo*. The traditional tools for splicing, editing, dubbing and so on, which had remained largely outside the possibilities of amateur media production in an analogue world, are now available at almost zero cost with digital media. The sharing was free. There is now a growing collection of tools[48] for remixing ready-made video, sound, image and text and for all abilities.

More elaborate mixing of digital materials using Web-based tools is also possible at marginal or zero cost. The concept of the 'web mashup' is a website or application that combines disparate data from different sources in ways that enable users to do new things or old things with a new efficiency. These new services are becoming more and more common as we use school Web portals or home pages that combine information from the library, student events, podcasts and relevant news sources. The BBC home page mashes up its content in this way according to the geographical location of the computer accessing it. *My Local Crime*[49] uses data from the UK's national crime database and plots it on to *Google* maps. What is emerging is a vast number of new ways of collating and presenting multiple layers of information in powerful visual forms. The *Programmable Web*[50] hosts a collection of over 5,000 mashups with an average of three new ones added daily.

In 2007, a teacher of literature, Jerome Burg, created a website called *Google Lit Trips*, which enables journeys from works of literary travel to be plotted on to *Google Earth*.[51] What emerge are literary road trips that mix the interactive satellite imagery of *Google Earth* with multimedia information about the literary work. One of the Lit Trips on the site is Amir's journey back to Afghanistan as described in the novel *The Kite Runner*. When students follow this trip they navigate using placemarks, created by Burg, which relate to specific chapters in the novel. They can zoom in to those places, tilt the view to see the terrain or examine buildings in 3D. Each placemark can be clicked to access a pop-up window that contains supplementary information – perhaps a photograph of a bazaar with an accompanying description from the book, or information about the Pashtun and links to information about Shia and Sunni Muslims. These windows can contain a variety of multimedia content including questions and/ or tasks for students to complete.

While Burg has made a number of Lit Trips, his site is open to others to make their own and share with the community of users. Students of all ages are contributing and many class projects involve pupils creating collaborative trips. Because *Google Lit Trips* uses .kmz files, the mashup only works inside *Google Earth*, pulling information into that platform from other data sets as instructed by the user. A browser-based mashup along the same principle, designed by Kazumi Atsuta and Thomas Sturm, is *MapSkip*, where anyone can create a weave of stories about places in their lives.[52] Places on *Google* maps can be marked up with stories, photographs and even sounds. The weaves are shared, rated and discussed by users of the site. Historical accounts, soundscapes, poetry, personal reflections and social change writings are some of the weaves currently available in and around the city of London and the Thames. Many have been contributed by school groups.

Practical task

The least daunting way of building your own mashup is to create a custom map with *Google* maps. This is a map on to which you can mark your favourite places, highlight walking routes or annotate points of interest with explanatory text, as well as add photographs and videos. The completed map mashup can then be embedded in a class blog, a VLE or simply shared through its URL. Follow the simple step-by-step video tutorial (http://maps.google.com/help/maps/mymaps/create.html or http://econym.org.uk/gmap) to create your map.

Perhaps the most powerful component of mashups, as we have seen, is their potential for collaboration. Now that you have your personal, custom map, begin to invite collaborators. On *Google* maps this is very straightforward. Simply click the 'Collaborate' link and invite those people you want to help create the map. You now have a team of 'reporters' who can mark, annotate and add photographs and videos to the map.

How could such a mashup, and the process used to create it, be used in your classroom? How could such an activity cross curriculum lines and become a whole school activity? Map mashup collaborations can also lead to direct engagement with the community at large. What local issues might benefit from a map mashup built from the collective collaboration of parents, teachers and pupils?

Ethical reflection: ownership and copyright

As we have seen consistently in these chapters, the Web has become a space for creation, collaboration and participation. The overwhelming driver of this culture has been the architecture of the Web itself, an architecture that favours openness and sharing. Whether a blog post, tweet or video, we are encouraged to share and re-purpose the work of others. The kinds of creative work that this can engender can be positive, for example in challenging the media monopolies in healthy ways. The Bush/Blair love duet mashup[53] or recut film trailers[54] give creative outlet to subversive voices that reveal the inner workings and biases of the media products that surround us.

However, such products also challenge the notions of ownership and authority and raise questions about their status in an online world. Who owns the Bush/Blair mashup? Who has the authority to say how or where it might be used and who might use it? In other words, every time we create something and share it on the Web, do we have authority over it or is the process of sharing it a de facto renunciation of that authority? Once on the Web, is it a question of 'let the people do what the people will do' or can we make legitimate claims? Indeed, the idea of trying to stop such re-purposing might seem impossible. With a little ingenuity, anything in digital form can be copied, shared and re-purposed. For millions of people, the Internet means endless copies of free music, videos and other forms of entertainment. The difference between spreading culture and infringing copyright online has become blurred.

The topic of ownership and copyright is a notorious legal minefield and we can offer only a very broad brushstroke here. The battle lines are often drawn between those protecting the rights of individuals and businesses over their intellectual property through copyright laws and patents and those who think such laws are antithetical to the kinds of innovation that can take place through sharing and reuse. As we have seen, the Digital Economy Act is trying to introduce the means whereby copyright infringement can be more carefully policed through Internet service providers in the UK. Big media corporations have lobbied for Digital Resource Management (DRM) software and copy protection in order to protect copyright, an initiative that has been supported by the Digital Millenium Copyright Act in the US.

On the other side of the divide lie those who subscribe to a politics of openness. This position can be traced back to the counterculture movement of the 1960s and is often summarised with the slogan 'information wants to be free' – not free in the sense of price but in the sense of being free to copy and adapt to different uses.[55] The underlying idea is that useful information is the patrimony of humanity and that placing it under some form of protection (copyright or patent) is unethical. That position has been refined in a number of 'copyleft' movements over the past 25 years, including a number of licences created by Creative Commons, a non-profit organisation that was founded in 2001 by Harvard Professor of Law, Lawrence Lessig.[56]

The novelty introduced with these licences is that they allow an author to surrender some rights under copyright law in order that others can engage in creative activities with the work that would normally be reserved by the holder of the copyright. So, for example, music published with *Jamendo* with Creative Commons non-commercial licences can be remixed, re-purposed and shared for non-commercial purposes. *Wikipedia* uses a Creative Commons share-alike licence, which means that any work or derivative work may be published on the site if, and only if, it is released under the same licence. Many writers are now releasing their work using such licensing. Cory Doctorow, who we met in Chapter 2, says of Creative Commons:

> CC lets me be financially successful, but it also lets me attain artistic and ethical success. Ethical in the sense that CC licenses give my readers a legal framework to do what readers have always done in metaspace: pass the works they love back and forth, telling each other stories the way humans do. Artistic because we live in the era of copying, the era when restricting copying is a fool's errand, and by CC gives me an artistic framework to embrace copying rather than damning it.

(2007)

However, not everyone is as positive as Doctorow. While Creative Commons licences might be making it safer to copy, remix and share, many believe that it is reinforcing the idea that 'the reward for Web-work is at best attention and recognition and at worst the exploitation of vulnerable labour' (Lanier 2010: 196). For every Cory Doctorow there are thousands, possibly hundreds of thousands, who are doing such work for free and/or watching any value that their work might have accrued being siphoned off by the contextual ads accompanying those search engines that index and retrieve that work.

These are some of the issues in ownership and copyright that we need to keep in our minds as we participate in digital networks. The challenge is not only to recognise the need for appropriate copyright as an ethical act and as protection against commercial exploitation. In a culture where immediate access to digital artefacts is expected, there is also a need to cultivate an ethics of ownership in terms of respect and responsibility. As we take what someone has produced as 'ours' with no recognition of the gift, we lose the sense of gifting something that we have produced and that is ours to gift. That ethics of reciprocity and restraint needs to be reinforced. Not only is it increasingly important in an online world, it is vital in all the worlds we live in.

Reflective task

Issues of ownership and copyright have an interesting parallel to the world of assessment and qualifications. As notions of ownership become blurred, it becomes harder to identify and assess the contributions of various individuals. Does this matter? How might an alternative approach to assessment, reward and qualification be constructed that builds on social media's inherent potential for collaboration, copy, remix and sharing?

Summary

This chapter has taken four key themes (playing, exploring, reflecting and expressing) and looked at how they can be explored through various networked digital technologies. Along the way, we have also explored a range of ethical issues associated with such technologies and their use, both privately and within educational settings. We have given examples of projects drawn from different settings, including schools and wider life, which, we hope, have usefully illustrated some of the educational potential of such approaches.

The impacts of these processes and technologies on education in today's schools are somewhat limited. What we hope to do in our final chapter is move our practice forwards in different ways: first, by using some tools that have recently been published to help us imagine new possibilities for education; second, by considering some practical technologies that are available today to help you inform and organise your own work as a teacher more effectively.

Discussion points

■ We clearly live in a resource-rich environment. We are all (inveterate or not) collectors of information. What are some suggestions you could make for increasing the pooling of the collective resources of your school?

■ What channels do schools currently offer for the discussion of the ethical implications of Web-based learning? Could they be increased? If so, how would you set about doing so?

Useful websites/resources

http://cooltoolsforschools.wikispaces.com   Web 2.0: Cool Tools for Schools

www.classroom20.com   *Classroom 2.0*, the social network for those interested in Web 2.0 and social media in education

www.educause.edu/resources   Educause Resource Center

Notes

1 www.education.gov.uk/ukccis
2 www.education.gov.uk/ukccis/strategy/research
3 http://clickcleverclicksafe.direct.gov.uk
4 http://thinkuknow.co.uk/teachers
5 http://childnet-int.org/safety/teachers.aspx
6 Available from http://simulationtrainingsystems.com
7 www.guardian.co.uk/technology/2011/mar/11/i-was-games-addict
8 www.bbc.co.uk/news/uk-england-devon-12687039
9 www.walesonline.co.uk/news/health-news/2101/04/05teeth-take-a-hit-when-computer-games-lead-to-bad-bites-91466-26174981
10 http://eu.battle.net/wow/en/
11 www.clubpenguin.com/

12 www.kzero.co.uk/universe.php
13 www.yoyogames.com/gamemaker
14 http://secondlife.com
15 http://incrediland
16 www.delicious.com
17 www.diigo.com
18 www.furl.com
19 http://ratemyprofessors.com
20 http://technorati.com/
21 http://edublogs.org
22 http://studentchallenge.edublogs.org
23 www.radiowaves.co.uk
24 http://educationblogawards.org/postiveandpowerful/
25 http://year5.ferrylane.net/2011/02/08/more-than-just-a-website-by-sharon/
26 www.myspace.com
27 www.bebo.com
28 www.linkedin.com
29 http://multiply.com
30 www.ning.com
31 www.learncentral.org
32 www.classroom20.com
33 http://edubuzz.org
34 www.schoolofeverything.com
35 www.kazaa.com
36 www.limewire.com
37 www.bittorrent.com
38 www.jamendo.com
39 www.spotify.com
40 www.flickr.com
41 www.deviantart.com
42 www.slideshare.com
43 http://academicearth.com
44 http://videolectures.net
45 www.youtube.com
46 www.vimeo.com
47 www.youtube.com/watch?v=6gmP4nk0EQOE
48 See for example, http://wwwgo2web2.0.net
49 http://mylocalcrime.com
50 www.programmableweb.com/mashups
51 www.googlelittrips.com
52 www.mapskip.com
53 www.youtube.com/watch?v=UTEH6wZXPA4
54 www.youtube.com/watch?v=zZ2H37m_Yt8
55 The slogan is attributed to Stewart Brand, an iconic counterculture figure of the 1960s.
56 www.creativecommons.org

References

Becta (2006) *Computer Games in Education Report*. Available online: http://partners.becta.org.uk/index.php?section=rh (accessed 9 May 2011).

boyd, d. (2010) 'Making sense of privacy and publicity', keynote speech presented at SXSW, Austin, Texas, 13 March.

Clark, C. and Dugdale, G. (2009) *Young People's Writing: Attitudes, behaviour and the role of technology*, National Literacy Trust. Available online: www.literacytrust.org.uk/assets/0000/0226/Writing_survey_2009.pdf (accessed 9 May 2011).

Greenhow, C. M. (2011) 'Re-writing community and literacies among U.S. teens in social network sites', paper accepted for presentation at the Computer-assisted Learning Conference (CAL) 2011: Learning Futures: Education, Technology and Sustainability, Manchester, April 13–15.

Hoofnagle, C. J., King, J., Li, S. and Turow, J. (2010) 'How different are young adults from older adults when it comes to information privacy attitudes and policies?', Social Science Research Network, 14 April. Available online: http://ssrn.com (accessed 9 May 2011).

Huizinga, J. (1955) *Homo ludens: A study of the play-element in culture*, Boston, MA: Beacon Press.

ipoque (2006) 'New ipoque survey confirms the continuing boom of P2P file sharing'. Available online: www.ipoque.com/news-and-events/news/pressrelease-ipoque-241006.html (accessed 9 May 2011).

Jenkins, H. (2011) 'How learners can be on top of their game: an interview with James Paul Gee (part one)', Confessions of an Aca/Fan. Available online: http://henryjenkins.org/2011/03/how_learners_can_be_on_top_of.html (accessed 9 May 2011).

Keen, A. (2007) *The Cult of the Amateur: How today's Internet is killing our culture and assaulting our economy*, London: Nicholas Brealey.

Lanier, J. (2010) *You Are Not a Gadget: A manifesto*, London: Penguin.

Lemuel, J. (2006) 'Why I registered on Facebook', *The Chronicle of Higher Education Careers Online*. Available online: http://chronicle.com/jobs/news/2006/09/2006090101c/printable.html (accessed 9 May 2011).

Livingstone, S., Haddon, L., Görzig, A. and Ólafsson, K. (2011) *Risks and Safety for Children on the Internet: The UK report*. Available online: http://eprints.lse.ac.uk/33730/ (accessed 9 May 2011).

Maloney, E. (2007) 'What Web 2.0 can teach us about learning', *The Chronicle of Higher Education*. Available online: http://chronicle.com/article/What-Web-20-Can-Teach-Us/8332 (accessed 9 May 2011).

Mazer, J. P., Murphy, R. E. and Simonds, C. J. (2007) 'I'll see you on "Facebook": the effects of computer-mediated teacher self-disclosure on student motivation, affective learning, and classroom climate, *Communication Education*, 56: 1–17.

Peters, I. (2009) *Folksonomies: Indexing and retrieval in Web 2.0 (knowledge and information)*, Berlin: De Gruyter.

Powers, E. (2007) 'A lesson in viral video', *Inside Higher Ed*, 7 February. Available online: www.insidehighered.com/news/2007/02/07/web (accessed 9 May).

Rushkoff, D. (2011) *Program or Be Programmed: Ten commands for a digital age*, New York: Or Books.

Steinkuehler, C. (2008) 'Massively multiplayer online games as an educational technology: an outline for research', *Educational Technology*, 48(1): 10–21.

Sullivan, A. (2008) 'Why I blog', *The Atlantic*. Available online: www.theatlantic.com/magazine/archive/2008/11/why-i-blog/7060/ (accessed 9 May 2011).

Surowiecki, J. (2005) *Wisdom of Crowds*, New York: Anchor Books.

Sykes, J., Oskoz, A. and Thorne, S. (2008) 'Web 2.0, synthetic immersive environments and mobile resources for language education, *CALICO Journal*, 25: 528–46.

Wastiau, P., Kearney, C. and van den Berghe, W. (2009) 'How are digital games used in schools?', in Alexa, J. and Gerhard, P. (eds) *Evaluation*, Brussels: European Schoolsnet.

Wesch, M. (2007) 'The machine is us/ing us final version', *Digital Ethnography*, 8 March. Available online: http://mediatedcultures.net/ksudigg/?p=84 (accessed 9 May 2011).

Williamson, B. (2009) *Computer Games, Schools and Young People*, Bristol: Futurelab.

7 Moving forwards and conclusion

Key questions

- What does the future for education hold?
- What will be the role of technology in this?
- How can I best prepare myself for a long and happy career teaching with technology?

We hope that this book has taken you on a new journey through the fields of social media, digital networked technology and education. Working together on this book has been a journey for us too. Congratulations on getting to the final chapter! As you will discover, this chapter is slightly different from the ones that have preceded it. Here, we are seeking to help you plan ahead for your use of technology throughout the next part of your teaching career. For those of you undertaking initial teacher education, this will see you move into your NQT year; for those more experienced teachers, we hope that the following ideas, frameworks and activities will assist in your future development.

In our experience, looking ahead and trying to second-guess developments in the world of technology or education is always difficult (and potentially dangerous). Winston Churchill once quipped that 'it is always wise to look ahead but difficult to look further than you can see' (BrainyQuote 2011). But, while it might be difficult and potentially dangerous, we believe that it is a valuable exercise when done in the right way.

In this chapter, we will build on the work of others who have attempted to map out the future territory of education and the role that technology might play within it. We will then attempt to link some of these ideas to your own work today, as an individual working within a specific school and subject area. However, before we proceed, we should state our provisos.

First, looking ahead at future scenarios for education and technology should not be done in order to try to pinpoint specific developments, technologies or ideas. Predicting things at that micro level is a pointless exercise. So, looking ahead and trying to map general directions of travel is the best option. This is what we will be doing here.

Second, linked to this is that we should look ahead to, and ultimately plan for, different types of scenarios. Covering all the bases is a good strategy. While we may have our own particular 'favourites' or preferred futures (all things being equal), prioritising these and allowing them to prevent a broader range of thought about alternative scenarios is risky and can lead to us being at best disappointed and unprepared, and at worst marginalised and ignored.

Third, adopting a range of lenses or filters through which to consider future scenarios is likely to be a useful strategy. To take a metaphor from the world of photography, some types of lenses will allow wider viewpoints to be established, while others will allow for greater focus or clarity on a particular object; some filters enhance natural light, while others impose and manipulate light for different purposes. This metaphor applies to how we think about future developments and can give us alternative ways of thinking or looking. We need to look ahead in different ways and with different tools.

Finally, there is real strength in doing this type of activity together. You are probably reading this book on your own somewhere. But make a commitment to talk through your ideas in response to this chapter with friends or colleagues. The wisdom of the crowd can be very powerful!

Looking ahead: *Beyond Current Horizons*

One of the most recent, and extensive, pieces of research into the future of education and technology was *Beyond Current Horizons* (Futurelab/DCSF 2010). The aim of the *Beyond Current Horizons* research project was:

> to explore the potential futures for education that might emerge at the intersection of social and technological change over the coming two decades. Its purpose is to map out current and emerging socio-technical trends, the critical uncertainties in our understanding of future socio-technical developments, and the challenges or opportunities that such developments might offer to educators.
>
> (ibid.)

Beyond Current Horizons is probably the largest piece of research done into educational futures in recent years. As such, it provides a wealth of interesting data about future scenarios for education. In particular, it developed six scenarios. We will use these to structure a two-part task that we hope you will engage with. The first part can be done while you are reading the scenarios; the second part will need you to take some time out from reading this chapter and consider some wider questions.

Within the *Beyond Current Horizons* project, three future worlds were imagined. These worlds were given the following descriptive titles:

1   Trust yourself;
2   Loyalty points;
3   Only connect.

Within each world, two future scenarios for education were explored. These scenarios, informed by the thinking of educationalists, sociologists, futurologists and others, provide a fascinating insight into potential futures. Remember, these are not predictions. Rather, they are deliberately provocative and designed to promote discussion. As you read them, you may find that you are drawn towards particular ideas, values or positions. We would suggest that this is quite normal. However, other people will be drawn to alternatives and this can lead to fruitful discussions.

Practical task A

The *Beyond Current Horizons* website (Futurelab/DCSF 2010) provides extensive details about each of these worlds and their scenarios. There is also a separate *Vision Mapper* website (Futurelab 2010) that allows you to explore them further through a range of practical activities. The scenario summaries provided below are paraphrased from this site.

As you read through each summary, pick out some key points regarding:

■   the organisation of the educational system in each scenario;

■   the role of the teacher and the skills they might need in each scenario;

■   how learners are described and what they are required to do in each scenario;

■   any other key themes that strike you as relevant or interesting.

World 1: Trust yourself

Scenario 1: Informed choice

In this scenario, the state has gradually withdrawn from educational provision and regulation. It has been left with a small role in the provision of early years and primary education, and also ensures that systems are in place to allow individuals to navigate a more complex educational landscape of provision.

Beyond primary education, individuals and employers fund learning offerings that are available in a range of sites, such as workplaces, homes, local communities and educational institutions. Personalised, wearable technologies allow individuals to access educational resources in multiple sites, enabling them to 'wrap' educational provision around their needs and preferences.

Mentors are at the heart of educational decision-making. They are recruited by the student to help them build a coherent educational trajectory and to make informed choices from the range of offerings. The mentor and student have to work together closely in selecting and tailoring educational experiences that build on the student's personal history, strengths, background and experiences. Specific educators that the learner has chosen to work with tailor their educational offerings specifically around the needs and histories of the individual, supported in this by the information and advice offered by the learning mentor.

Within this scenario assessment processes build a picture of a learner's personal development over time and bring together the diverse elements of the individual's learning career in a coherent fashion. Advanced e-portfolios that intelligently combine information are a key tool to support this personal narrative.

Scenario 2: Independent consumers

In this scenario the state has withdrawn from providing any education provision after primary schooling. This has resulted in the abolishment of the National Curriculum, Ofqual and Ofsted, and has led to a dramatic change in the way education works. It has also placed sole responsibility on individuals, or their parents and guardians, to manage and determine their own educational decisions.

After primary school, education is funded by individuals and employers through 'learning offerings'. These offerings are available in a range of sites such as workplaces, homes, local communities and educational institutions. Like the previous scenario, wearable technologies allow the learner to access educational resources in a range of settings and differentiate these according to their individual needs or requirements.

Individuals have access to a 'catalogue' or 'online marketplace' of educational choices. They can make choices from the various items and are responsible for how these fit together into a coherent framework that meets their personal needs. The teaching that is delivered within these settings does not focus on an individual's history or life experience. Rather, it is characterised by standardised, expert pedagogies with uniform delivery. This allows potential students to know exactly what it is they are 'buying' each time.

So, individuals make their own educational decisions and create their own personal trajectories. They are helped, as required, by family and friends. Educational decisions may be based on immediate needs and interests, with no requirement to take account of past history or long-term future trajectories.

In this scenario, assessment is primarily about certification. It demonstrates the attainment of particular skills and competencies. The resulting lists of qualifications allow individuals to demonstrate their abilities to employers and make the move from education into employment.

World 2: Loyalty points

Scenario 3: Discovery

Within this scenario, education helps students to understand the diverse communities within which they might work, learn and live. In particular, it helps them to understand how they might make effective and valued contributions to these different settings. Learners are encouraged to become self-aware and expert participators in these communities, and to explore actively where they might want to learn and work.

Over time, each individual gains experiences of learning in a range of different organisations (some private, some public, some third sector). In each set of experiences, they will be encouraged to reflect upon how these different organisations shape the knowledge and the skills that are valued. Each organisation's set of curricular arrangements is publicly available for comparison and learners are encouraged to combine different elements according to their own interests. Teachers know that the knowledge they are sharing comes from a specific community. Therefore, they will encourage learners to discuss and debate it in various ways, contribute new ideas to it, and develop new ways of using it.

In this scenario, assessment is focused upon developing an individual's understanding. It aims to help them discover and reflect on their personal attributes and talents, and explore how these might contribute to different organisations and communities. Personal profiles will allow individuals to build 'reputation' indicators from their collaborators, offering peer reviews and other sophisticated data-tracking linked to the various learning activities that they have been involved in.

Scenario 4: Diagnosis

Within this scenario, education in all phases is delivered primarily through commercial or third-sector organisations, with businesses, social enterprises and faith groups all providing educational offerings that are tied to their economic, social or religious agendas. There is some minimal state provision for those with insufficient resources or 'talents' to enter other educational institutions.

As all educational institutions are closely tied to the life of commercial, not-for-profit, faith and other organisations, they use the educational frameworks that they provide to identify and train future members of the organisation. Individuals who demonstrate a particular set of skills that are desirable to an organisation are actively recruited, often at a young age, and then trained to meet the needs of the organisation. Employees have access to other forms of ongoing training and development through in-house 'schools' and 'universities'.

In all education institutions, teachers make an early diagnosis of a student's individual strengths. They match these to a required role in the relevant business, enterprise or religious programme. In summary, learning is all about preparing students for a particular function through a personalised and individual set of learning experiences.

In this scenario, assessment is highly personalised. It tracks the continued progress of the individual towards their future role. Success outcomes are judged by the extent to which the individual develops their skills in ways that are closely matched to the needs of the organisation. There will be many different assessment approaches, many of which are specific to the individual organisation. As a consequence, the name of the organisation that trains an individual will take on as much significance as the actual information provided by the assessment itself.

World 3: Only connect

Scenario 5: Integrated experience

In this scenario, education is seen as the collective responsibility of individuals, families, communities, businesses and the state. It is integrated into all areas of an individual's economic, social, leisure and personal life. Education and living are rarely separated. Instead, personal development, supporting the learning and development of others, and reflecting on the contribution of such learning to group progress, are all integral parts of how an individual functions within a specific community.

Apart from early years education, learning is not associated with specific periods of life or specific 'separate' locations. Rather, it is seen as an activity that individuals and groups participate in on an ongoing or as-required basis. The state still has an important role to play in making available and visible to all the opportunity to move between different communities, to take on new 'apprentice' roles in different communities, and to reflect upon the different knowledge and skills required to participate in different communities. Experts in different communities have a role to play in engaging newcomers to their communities, in making their knowledge more widely available, and in finding ways to foster collaborations across different 'subjects' or 'disciplines'.

Within this scenario, assessment is focused on providing feedback to groups rather than individuals. It provides details about their overall progress and achievement against meaningful goals. As a consequence of this, individuals do not talk about their own 'qualifications', but rather about their contribution to significant events, breakthroughs, contributions and performances.

Scenario 6: Service and citizenship

In this final scenario, education is predominantly the responsibility of the state and the individual, with the state seen as responsible for 'shaping citizens' who are able to take on appropriate roles and perform appropriate behaviours in the diverse communities and settings outside formal education.

This state provision of formal education is clearly separated from the rest of society and is perceived as being an essential prerequisite for active participation within the real world (i.e. the world beyond education). Education is characterised by a focus on 'civic participation' and the development of specific skills and competencies for the workforce and community. Considerable emphasis is given to the value of thinking and acting communally.

Teachers have a responsibility to prepare individuals for participation and collaboration within their communities. Their work focuses specifically on a standardised competency-based approach, developing problem-solving, collaboration and thinking skills. There is a limited attempt to provide more than an introduction to the 'basics' of different subject domains, as knowledge is seen as collaboratively produced and rapidly changing in the 'real world' outside schools.

Within this scenario assessment charts individual learners' capacities to perform in collective and group settings, and is used to predict individuals' capacity to take on different types of roles in these settings.

Planning ahead

In Practical task A you were asked to read the six scenarios (each one paraphrased from the *Vision Mapper* website) and identify key points in respect of four key areas:

- the organisation of the educational system in each scenario;
- the role of the teacher and the skills they might need in each scenario;
- how learners are described and what they are required to do in each scenario;
- any other key themes that strike you as relevant or interesting.

Take some time now to review your points. Try to organise them into groups (using the above four headings or other headings of your own that seem suitable). Having done that, compare them to our responses in Table 7.1.

You will have noticed an additional column in Table 7.1. Alongside our key points (and sub-points), there are a number of questions and comments. We wrote these down as we reflected on the key points that we had drawn from the six scenarios. These questions may be useful to you as you consider the second half of this two-part task.

TABLE 7.1 Key points from the *Beyond Current Horizons* scenarios

Key point	Comments and indicative questions
Community	
Relationships	How do relationships within communities facilitate engagement with education? How do the demands of the individual learner equate to those of the community? What happens when there is conflict?
Reputation	Should future educational systems identify and reward learners' reputations within communities? (link to 'Assessment' below)
Civic	Civic responsibilities and promotion feature strongly in some scenarios. At what level (surface, deep, etc.) should these inform curriculum planning and learning opportunities?
Access	
Terms	Who decides who has access to what?
Location	Where can education be accessed from?
Roles and responsibilities	
Power and authority	Who decides what individuals or groups should do for their education? How are people or groups held accountable to the education choices they make, or the educational processes they engage in?
Curriculum	
Subjects/disciplines	Are individual subjects or disciplines important enough to keep?
Organisation	How should individual pieces of knowledge be put together to form established curricula? Who owns these curricula? What or whose purpose should they serve?
Difference	What happens when people or groups disagree about what is important in a particular curriculum area? Should, or how can, notions of 'difference' be accommodated or celebrated?
Knowledge	
Value	What value does knowledge have? Who decides what it is valuable to know or not?
Process or product	Is it important to know things? Or is it better to know how to know things? Or is it both? How are the two linked (if at all)?
Teachers	
Role	What is the role of a teacher in all this?
Pedagogy	What skills or attributes would a teacher have in these different scenarios?

TABLE 7.1 continued

Key point	Comments and indicative questions
Expertise	Is it important that a teacher has a specific expertise? Should this limit their involvement in other areas, i.e. those areas outside their area of expertise? Is the role of 'expert' about sharing knowledge? Or is it about facilitating access to knowledge? Or is it both?
Mentor	How would the role of 'mentor' relate to that of 'teacher'?
Choice	
Learner	How much freedom should learners have in choosing what to study?
Location	Given multiple locations in which learning can take place, what should inform the choices learners make in where to learn?
Qualification	
Type	What will qualifications look like in the future?
Value	What value will they have in terms of personal, social or other forms of development?
Ownership	Who 'owns' a qualification? Will it always be an individual? Can groups or communities be rewarded by qualifications based on their communal efforts?
Assessment	
Knowledge, skills and competencies	What should we be assessing in the future?
Value	Linked to 'Qualifications' above, where will value be found in the assessment process and who will 'own' it? Who will be rewarded by it?
Purpose	What will the outcomes of assessment be used for? Personal advancement? Civic benefit?
Individuality	
Differentiation	Will teachers/mentors have a role to play in differentiating curriculum opportunities? Can this be done in other ways?
Personalisation	How will individuals' life stories and prior experiences shape their engagement with educational opportunities? How will elements of discovery or diagnosis help shape educational opportunities for the individual in such a way that empowers them for their future work, life, contribution to society, etc?

Practical task B

For the second half of this task, we would like you to consider the roles that technology might play in these future scenarios. Using the key points that you collected in the first part of the task, and perhaps the ones that we collected too, together with the questions in Table 7.1, consider the following:

- Are there specific technologies that I know about today that might be able to help support the future of education as outlined within these scenarios?

- What combinations of technologies might need to be brought together in order to support some of these new scenarios?

- As a teacher (and we will presume that you will still have a role of some sort in the future!), what sort of technological skills or knowledge will I need to support my work?

- Are there aspects of current pedagogy that will either (1) be redundant, or (2) be enhanced, or (3) be completely different in the future?

Beyond Current Horizons emphasises our core belief that developments in technology and education are interrelated and take place in a broad context. It is vital that we do not take either education or technology and consider developments therein in isolation from each other or this broader context.

Equipping yourself for the future

The second half of this chapter will be much more personal. In it, we are going to do two things. First, we will discuss a way of using a simple technology to help keep track of your digital life; second, we will explore a short set of concluding ideas for what you can do now to help prepare yourself for your future education career, whatever changes lie around the corner.

Using RSS to glue your digital life together

As you adopt digital networked technologies within your personal and professional life, it is highly likely that you will be undertaking a range of activities. These might include:

- reading blog posts;

- getting the latest podcasts;

- tracking favourite tags;

- engaging in *Twitter* conversations;

- commenting on various sites;

- reading articles from online newspapers, forums, magazines and journals;

- monitoring changes to wiki pages and websites;

- sharing photographs stored in *Flickr*;

- and much more besides!

How can you keep track of them all? From loosely connected pieces of technology are we simply creating loosely connected 'deafening noise'? There is one more piece in the puzzle, however, which connects the pieces together and which can act as a conduit through which the deafening noise can be filtered to create a more harmonious music.

Instead of visiting all the sites you are interested in on a regular basis, you can subscribe to those sites using an RSS 'reader' or 'aggregator', which checks them for updates and automatically downloads new content. RSS (sometimes referred to as 'really simple syndication') is the glue that ties together the various pieces, filters the content that we want to receive and pipes it to us collected in one place.

As authors, our experiences with RSS began with our desire to keep up to date with the growing number of blogs we read. We started to subscribe to blogs and read updates in *Google Reader*. We made sure that others could subscribe to our own blogs through their RSS feeds. We experimented. The photographs of vintage bicycles that we discussed in Chapter 2 were updated regularly. They offered an RSS feed button, which meant that new photographs could appear in *Google Reader* without the need to constantly check *Flickr*. We subscribed to feeds offered by newspapers, filtering the information according to our interests at particular times. We subscribed to podcasts and began to aggregate our most important tags from such silos as *delicious* and *YouTube*.

As we began incorporating blogs into our teaching, we subscribed to student blogs as well as to the comments that they received on their posts. We could monitor their posts and the conversations that were taking place around them. Searching the Web, we often use the same search query. We created 'alerts' in *Google* for persistent searches, which through RSS were fed into our *Reader*. As we read our content in *Google Reader* we began to share items we thought would be interesting to others and we subscribed to the shared items of colleagues and friends.

We became familiar with the form and function of a technology that pulls information into a central repository or database. We curated the feeds that we collected by filtering and refining them constantly in a process similar to that described in our discussion of using *Twitter*. Our repository itself became searchable as *Google Reader* included a search facility on one or more feeds. We now have a dynamic archive of items that can be mined for information as and when we need it and the results can be shared with others.

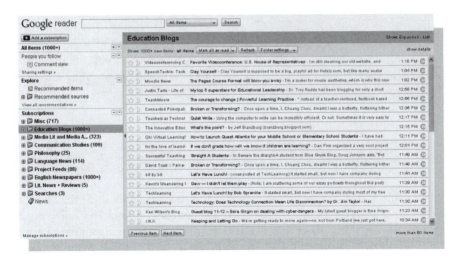

Figure 7.1 Snapshot of author's *Google Reader* account

Search, collect, sort, curate and share. We were slowly developing our literacy with online information tools, the central conduit of which was, and is, RSS. With our *Reader* constantly detecting information in the background, we were confident that we had in place a radar that was identifying items that deserved our attention and that gave us the possibility of sharing our discoveries.

At the level of our personal learning, we soon realised that we were developing personal knowledge management systems that harnessed the power of machines with the power of the socialising component of the emerging technologies that we have discussed in this book. In doing so, we also realised that such a system could be used for managing resources and learning conversations in our teaching.

Practical task

Have you ever used an RSS aggregation tool such as *Google Reader*? If not, why not take this opportunity to set up an account with *Google* and explore the potential of RSS to help organise your digital life?

Explore some of the functionality of the interface over the next few weeks. But keep in mind the following progression: search, collect, sort, curate and share. Don't forget that a tool is only as useful as the skill through which it is put to use. While you might find it easy to collect things, unless you are able to sort and curate them effectively you will quickly be swamped.

Furthermore, making that link to sharing is where your own work as a teacher in finding and preparing resources reaches out to your pupils. This is where the digital rubber hits the super-highway!

Conclusion

In concluding this book, we wanted to draw together some final advice from our experiences of teaching with technology in school and university. While there is always more that can be said, we hope that these thoughts, presented in no particular order, may help you in the next step of your teaching career with technology.

Understand the biases and set your own defaults

It is not essential to understand how a 2-litre turbo engine works in order to drive the car to work and back. We can use technologies without fully understanding them. However, we need to understand how certain technologies are biased towards certain behaviours.

Throughout this book we have seen how digital networked technologies are biased towards the social, towards sharing and towards participation. However, this is a specific kind of social. Most digital networked technologies are biased towards asynchronous communication at a distance: they allow enormous flexibilities in communicating with others when those others are not in the same room at the same time.

When we understand that, we can exploit it. We can use wikis to encourage collaborative writing when the pupils are in different places and are able to contribute at different times. We can use virtual worlds to enable pupils to come together in ways that simulate their coming together in a single room at a single moment in time.

If we fail to see this bias then the technology can begin to shape our behaviour in ways that it wants. There is something quite uncollaborative about studying in a virtual world while sitting in a classroom with 28 other students. There can be something uncommunicative about using *PowerPoint* in a small group seminar, something that distracts from the potential of the physical presence of the group and the communication that it can generate.

So, learn to question the assumptions and the defaults. Critique the biases of the technologies that you use in your teaching. Watch out for the amplifying tendencies that they all contain. Teach your pupils to do the same. As we suggested in Chapter 4, choose and use your technologies carefully.

Beware of what you give up

As I write this sentence a football match is about to begin on the television. I cannot write effectively and watch the football match at the same time. In fact, I cannot write effectively and listen to music at the same time. Music can never be sufficiently in the background so as not to distract me from reading and/or writing. So I make choices. I need to finish this piece of writing and the cost of not doing so (letting colleagues down, respecting contractual agreements) persuades me to turn the television off, turn the radio off and write. I have given something up that, on balance, is worth the cost.

Despite a number of claims about the merits of multitasking, doing one thing comes at the expense of doing something else. The same is true of any technology that we take time and effort to learn to use well. We both spent time learning how to use *Twitter* (sending a tweet is obviously easy, curating a personal/professional network with *Twitter* is much more difficult), time that we took away from other things that we attend to on a daily basis. We may blog less as a result. We may send fewer texts than we used to. We may walk the dogs less, or drink less beer. The point is that adopting a new technology means reducing the use of an old one. Sometimes it is not clear what exactly is given up (it was not initially clear that using *Twitter* would reduce blog posting), but something will be.

Using technology in the classroom (or indeed anywhere) means not doing something else in that context. We need to be as aware of what is given up as we are about what is gained in order to calculate the cost and make informed choices.

Learn to be a beginner

We recently heard the story of a father's experiences with his 4-year-old daughter. Sophie became fascinated with the iPad and would play with it at any opportunity. Her abilities with the technology flabbergasted her father. She picked up the simple visual and gestural controls and almost intuitively became adept at resizing photographs, making photo comic strips, recording her voice and adding it to images. New apps were like jelly to her, he told us – she gobbled them up.

As we heard about Sophie's experience and her behaviour with the iPad we were reminded of the Zen practice of *Shoshin*, which we came across in *Zen Mind, Beginner's Mind* (Suzuki and Dixon 1970). Translated as 'beginner's mind', *Shoshin* is an attitude of openness, eagerness and lack of preconceptions that it is possible to have as we approach any subject or idea at any level. *Shoshin* is an ability to see things always as fresh and new, an attitude that includes both doubt and possibility. In many ways we might expect Sophie to display beginner's mind. But Suzuki and Dixon's point is that, even if we have achieved an advanced knowledge of a subject, we can still approach it with beginner's mind in order to see the many possibilities that are open to discovery: 'In the beginner's mind there are many opportunities, but in the expert's there are few' (ibid.: 21).

Beginner's mind is a richer and more valuable perspective on learning and change than the one offered by the digital natives/immigrants debate that we critiqued in Chapter 3 (see pages 42–3). In the technological landscapes that we have been exploring in this book we will all, always, be novices or beginners. So we have to be good beginners and cultivate *Shoshin* in order to see the possibilities that are open to us through changing circumstances, tools and technologies. Good novices ask naive, 'silly' questions. They make stupid mistakes, move on from them quickly and take their learning with them. They ask for advice when they really need it. They give advice to others when others really need it. Any parent of very young children knows how much their children want to teach them. They want to teach because good beginners know that the best way to learn is to teach others just beyond that which they think they know.

So, learn to be a good beginner and mindful of staying one.

Learn to unlearn

Beginner's mind is perhaps more easily cultivated in the young because they have fewer preconceptions about the way the world might work and the place that they might inhabit in it. When Sophie started using the iPad, she approached it not as a laptop without a keyboard, nor as an iPhone without the need to reply. Had she done so she may have tried to import her habits from those devices to the new piece of technology. Using a mobile phone is not the same as using a landline. Each shapes different habits. Using *Twitter* is not the same as blogging. We learn new habits in part by unlearning old ones. The many people who, faced with *Twitter*, respond by saying 'I just don't get it', may be trying to equate the technology with habits and routines from another technology that just does not fit. Learning how to use something like *Twitter* is learning that *Twitter* is not a blogging tool, and it is not SMS. It is learning the habits of *Twitter*.

The law of unintended consequences drives much of the innovation that has seeped into our everyday digital worlds. Many of the ways in which digital networked communication tools are used were not predicted by those who initially designed them. The inventors of *Twitter* did not know how their tool would be used, how it might develop or what it might be good for. To find out they had to launch it and let people have a go. The same principle applies to the place of technology in our lives, personal and professional.

In order to evaluate a new tool for yourself or your students you have to try it out. Learn how to use it. Allow yourself to unlearn the old habits as you learn the new and appreciate that those new habits may be of little use with whatever comes next. These are vital steps before introducing a new technology into your classroom.

Unlearning old habits is the paradoxical challenge of learning new ones.

Be suspicious of 'walled gardens'

The 'music centre', an integrated system of record player, radio receiver, CD player and loudspeakers, became popular in the 1980s. While music aficionados and hi-fi enthusiasts tended to look down on integrated systems because of the compromises over quality in comparison to 'separates', I was reluctant to buy into the idea simply because, if one part of the system broke down, the whole thing had to be taken in to be repaired. It was a 'closed' system and often factory-sealed in ways that discouraged repair, tinkering or upgrading.

Since then I have remained suspicious of technologies that are hidden behind walls and always preferred systems that can be repaired, modified or 'hacked'. Often my technological skills are insufficient to make the repair myself or the modification that I imagine is possible, so I find someone who has those skills. The principle, however, guides my adoption of new tools, digital and analogue.

In education, the idea of the closed system, factory-sealed and protected, has manifested itself in such tools as 'course management systems'. Paradoxically, the technology that drives these systems, and that allows for the most widespread sharing of ideas, knowledge and expertise that we have ever known, is turned against itself to conceal and withhold such ideas, knowledge and expertise. The 'walled gardens' of these proprietary gated communities and knowledge repositories cannot be scaled. Instead, they require access rights, keys in the form of passwords and the permissions of their owners before we can benefit from their contents.

Perhaps because we started playing with computers when their components were 'separates' (the computer, the operating system and software, which we programmed to do the things we wanted to achieve), we realised very quickly that the 'walled gardens' were simply managerial software solutions to institutional organisation that serve a particular vision of education. Proprietary systems are about ownership; they have proprietors to whom, when we use them, we are answerable. The reason that such systems exist is, above all, to safeguard whatever is inside.

Clearly, many of the arguments for the 'walled garden', course management systems in schools are made with regard to the safety and privacy of the children who populate them, and these are legitimate concerns. Children and young people benefit from dedicated areas that are protected, whether from the traffic or from uninvited others. However, a more worrying argument hides beneath this and concerns the nature of teaching and learning. The course management system manifests the view that knowledge is a commodity that is owned and in need of protection.

But is knowledge really a commodity in the way that a bicycle is? If we give our bicycle away to Sophie, she benefits and we are reduced to walking. If we give our knowledge away to Sophie, however, she benefits and we lose nothing. Knowledge is not a commodity in the same way. Sharing knowledge, expertise and experience is the essence of education. Hiding it behind walled gardens is its nemesis.

Take a sabbatical

The Sabbath is a weekly day of rest and/or worship that has been adopted over hundreds of years by a variety of religions and for a variety of rituals. Sabbath years (every seventh), were mandated to allow the land to 'rest' and remain uncultivated by human hand. The Sabbath has a firm place in secular societies and within the weekly work cycle is seen to be a day for recreation and cultivating well-being. The practice of 'sabbatical leave', a one-year break from teaching and other duties to enable academics to write books and/or undertake research, owes it origin to the Sabbath year.

The Sabbath is a time of rest, a time for recovery from cultivation, a time to promote health and switch off. More recently, this idea of the Sabbath has been applied to technology. Virtual sabbaticals have been recommended recently in various online and offline media. The idea is that turning off can be liberating; that untying an electronic umbilical cord can allow a deeper exploration of those people and experiences that are perhaps most close.

So, leave your technological tools alone in your class on occasions. And leave technology alone in your lives sometimes. Perhaps do so once a week and call it a sabbatical.

Reflect on Thoreau's thought that the man who constantly and desperately keeps going to the post office to check for correspondence from others 'has not heard from himself in a long while' (Powers 2010).

Interrogate the hype

The amount of information on the Web about the nature of the Web is staggering. Reports, studies, discussions, rants, marketing, articles, publicity, statistics, insights and predictions are constant, and regularly spill over into print media to fuel talk about the impact that digital technology is having on all aspects of society. In many ways this is unsurprising. We are living in a world of technology very different from the one we grew up in. The technologies that the teenagers in our schools will use as adults have not been invented yet. That speed of change attracts attention and, with so much attention, the need to be attended to can result in hyped-up claims and counter-claims.

In various chapters of this book we have introduced a number of the most influential writers who have emerged on to this canvas during the past 10–15 years. Some are more optimistic about the impact of the Internet and digital networked technologies. They emphasise the participatory nature of the Internet, and how the 'global village' can facilitate liberation and empowerment and encourage a diversity of thought and expression. They look at how an abundance of information can lead to new opportunities for learning and help a growing number of people on the planet who are clamouring for education.

Others are more pessimistic. Instead, they emphasise that the Web polarises opinion and talk, encourages closed-minded sectarianism and mob rule, diminishes what it means to be human and imprisons us in a closed feedback loop. They emphasise the ways in which information overload is having a negative impact on learning and especially reading, and express a fear that the impact of digital education is an overall dumbing down of the population.

In these chapters we hope to have communicated a healthy scepticism to claims and counter-claims of this type, particularly in respect of the ways in which you choose and use technologies within your teaching. If we side towards being more optimistic than pessimistic, it is only because pragmatically we are now in a position to interrogate critically the claims both through more traditional literacy practices (particularly deep engagement and critical thinking skills) and by adopting the tools of online 'crap detection' (Rheingold 2009a) that are now available to us.

With a little licence, we can apply Newton's Third Law of Motion to online arguments: 'For every argument, there is an equal and opposite argument.' Interrogate the hype by finding both and examining each. Only then, having considered the various options, begin the process of using new technologies within your teaching.

Final words

So, with the thought of a digital sabbatical forefront in our minds, this book comes to an end. We hope that you have enjoyed the journey to this point. During your teaching career you will experience many changes. But we hope that the ideas, principles and practices that we have explored throughout this book will help you ensure that your pedagogy remains vibrant and contemporary in approach. Above all, we hope you will remain critical of the rhetoric that abounds in the fields of education and technology, but sympathetic and responsive to the opportunities that they present.

Discussion points

- Regardless of what the future holds, how can I best prepare myself for a productive teaching career that is characterised by a healthy scepticism towards technology while, simultaneously, exploiting its positive benefits?
- How can I find the time to initiate, develop and sustain a meaningful networked digital life that supports my professional practice and pedagogy?

Useful websites/resources

www.google.com/reader *Google Reader* home page

References

BrainyQuote (2011) 'Winston Churchill quotes'. Available online: www.brainyquote. com/quotes/quotes/w/winstonchu129821.html (accessed 15 December 2011).

Doctorow, C. (2007) *Commoner Letter #2*. Available online: http://creativecommons.org/ weblog/entry/7774 (accessed 4 May 2011).

Futurelab (2010) *VisionMapper*. Available online: www.visionmapper.org.uk (accessed 11 April 2011).

Futurelab/DCSF (Department for Children, Schools and Families) (2010) *Beyond Current Horizons*. Available online: www.beyondcurrenthorizons.org.uk (accessed 4 April 2011).

Powers, W. (2010) *Hamlet's BlackBerry: A practical philosophy for building a good life in the digital age*, New York: Harper.

Rheingold, H. (2009) 'Crap detection 101', SFGate Blogs. Available online: www.sfgate. com/cgi-bin/blogs/rheingold/detail?entry_id=42805 (accessed 9 May 2011).

Suzuki, S. and Dixon, T. (1970) *Zen Mind, Beginner's Mind*, New York: Walker/ Weatherhill.

Index

All Watched Over by Machines of Loving Grace (Brautigan) 5–6
Allison, Leslie 21–2, 23
'amateurization, mass' 28–9, 110–11
Arendt, Hannah 78

Bafa' Bafa' 102–3
Ballard, J. G. 19–20
'beginner's mind' 139–40
Beyond Current Horizons project 127–34
blogs 33–4, 112–14, 136; micro-blogs (*Twitter*) 21, 49–56, 108, 111–12, 140
bookmarks 108–9
Brautigan, Richard 5–6
Burg, Jerome 119

Carr, Nicholas 64, 72, 73–4
ccMixter 25–6
cognitive skills 63–4, 80
communities, social 34–5; *see also* social networking
context, importance of 60–1
copyright, online sharing 120–2
course management systems 141
Creative Commons 121–2
creativity 79–86, 91–7; social media examples 86–91
Croquelandia 104
crowd-sourcing 89, 92, 110–12
Csikszentmihalyi, Mihaly 80–1
curriculum development 10–11

delicious 108–9
Dewey Decimal Classification 107
digital animation 84
Digital Britain report 40
digital networked technologies 49, 126–7, 138–43; freeing of ownership 29–32; new ways of learning 25–9; organising with RSS 135–8; young people's use of 44–7; *see also* creativity; ethical issues; social networking
digital participation 38–41, 44–7; digital native/immigrant debate 41–4; and ethics of crowd-sourcing 110–12; *see also* literacies; social networking
Doctorow, Cory 19, 20–1, 23, 121
DropBox 84

education 1–2, 4, 126–7; new forms of 25–9; scenarios for the future 127–34; self-directed 8–9, 46–7; virtual 7–10, 12–15; *see also* technologies
educational blogging 113
Eliot, T. S. 65
Encyclopaedia Britannica 30–1
ethical issues: copyright, online sharing 120–2; and crowd-sourcing 110–12; game-worlds and identity 105–6; Internet safety/privacy 101, 116–17
ethnographic research 44–7, 104

Facebook 21–2, 34–5, 45, 47, 84, 88–9, 114–15, 117
Flickr 21, 26–7
folksonomic tagging 107–9
Furedi, Frank 62

gaming 82–3, 102–6
Gates, Bill 12
Gauntlett, David 85–6, 90, 96–7
Google 109, 119–20, 136–8
'Granny Cloud, The' 9
Greenfield, Patricia 64

Hanging Out, Messing Around, and Geeking Out (Ito) 44–7
hashtags 50, 53, 108

'Hole-in-the-Wall' project 7–10
Homo zappiens 42–3

identity, and game-worlds 105–6
information 32–5, 106; metadata 107–10;
    organising with RSS 135–8
information literacy 40–1, 48
interactive whiteboards (IWBs) 69–70
Ito, Mizuko 44–7

Jenkins, Henry 47–8

Keen, Andrew 110–11
Khan Academy 12–15
'knowledge economy' 39

language teaching, and *Twitter* 54–5
learning styles 43
libraries 107
literacies, media/information 40–1, 47–56

mashups 119–20
media production, pro/am 28–9, 110–11
metadata, information 107–10
micro-blogging *see Twitter*
Mitra, Sugata 7–10
MMORPGs 103–4, 106
mobile technologies 35, 45, 73–4, 115
motivation, intrinsic/extrinsic 93–4
music 25–6, 28, 83, 118

Napster 118
'Net Generation' 41–4
networks *see* digital networked
    technologies; social networking
Nietzsche, Friedrich 65–6

'overload', information 33–4
ownership of media 29–32, 120–2

photo-sharing 21, 26–7, 28
political context 1–2, 40–1
privacy, and social networking 116–17
professions 23–4; and 'amateurization'
    28–9, 110–11
publishing 23–4; and accuracy 31

Rheingold, Howard 51–2
RSS feeds 135–8

safety/privacy, Internet 101, 116–17
Script Frenzy 90–1
Scrivener 65
Second Life 104
self-directed learning 8–9, 46–7

sharing digital media 21, 26–7, 28, 84,
    118–20; and creativity 92, 94–5;
    ownership/copyright 120–2
Shirky, Clay 23–4, 87–8, 88–9
Shoshin 139–40
skills: cognitive 63–4, 80; technical 45–6;
    see also literacies
Skype, 'The Granny Cloud' 9
So You Want to ... sub-genre 21–2, 23
'social life' of information 33–4
social networking 33–4, 45, 53, 69,
    114–16; media literacies within 47–8,
    116–17; *see also Facebook*; *Twitter*
Steinkuehler, Constance 104
Stenhouse, Lawrence 10–11
Sullivan, Andrew 112–13
Sykes, Julie 104

tagging 50, 53, 107–9; ethics of crowd-
    sourcing 110–12
teachers 4, 10–11, 14–15, 23–4; and
    choice of technologies 62–7, 69–74, 78;
    and digital native/immigrant debate
    41–4; preparing for the future 135–43;
    and use of technologies 91–5
teaching materials, ownership of 29–32
technical skills 45–6
technologies 1–2, 5–7, 23–4; 'numbing'
    effect of 72, 73–4; scenarios for the
    future 127–34; teachers' choices 62–7,
    69–74, 78; young people's choices 67–9;
    see also digital networked technologies
Twitter 21, 50–6, 108, 111–12, 140
typewriters 65–6

Ushahidi 89, 92

video-sharing 21–2, 118–19; *see also*
    YouTube
virtual education: 'Hole-in-the-Wall'
    7–10; *Khan Academy* 12–15
virtual learning environments (VLEs) 63
virtual worlds 6, 102–6

Web 2.0 90, 110–11, 117, 118–19
web mashups 119–20
Wesch, Michael 118–19
Wikipedia 30–1, 32, 87–8, 92
writing 19–21, 23, 90–1, 113; and choice
    of technology 65–7

Xtranormal 21–2

YouTube 12–15, 21–2, 25, 28, 45, 90, 94